TEACH YOURSELF BOOKS

WRITING NON-FICTION
and getting published

D1408016

For UK order queries: please contact Bookpoint Ltd, 39 Milton Park, Abingdon, Oxon OX14 4TD. Telephone: (44) 01235 400414, Fax: (44) 01235 400454. Lines are open from 9.00–6.00, Monday to Saturday, with a 24 hour message answering service. Email address: orders@bookpoint.co.uk

For USA & Canada order queries: please contact NTC/Contemporary Publishing, 4255 West Touhy Avenue, Lincolnwood, Illinois 60646–1975, USA. Telephone: (847) 679 5500, Fax: (847) 679 2494.

Long renowned as the authoritative source for self-guided learning – with more than 30 million copies sold worldwide – the *Teach Yourself* series includes over 200 titles in the fields of languages, crafts, hobbies, sports, and other leisure activities.

A catalogue entry for this title is available from The British Library.

Library of Congress Catalog Card Number: On file

First published in UK 1998 by Hodder Headline Plc, 338 Euston Road, London, NW1 3BH.

First published in US 1998 by NTC/Contemporary Publishing, 4255 West Touhy Avenue, Lincolnwood (Chicago), Illinois 60646–1975 U.S.A.

Cover photo from Barbara Baran

Typeset by Transet Limited, Coventry, England.
Printed in Great Britain for Hodder & Stoughton Educational, a division of Hodder Headline Plc, 338 Euston Road, London NW1 3BH by Cox & Wyman Ltd, Reading, Berkshire.

Impression number   10 9 8 7 6 5 4 3 2 1
Year   2004 2003 2002 2001 2000 1999 1998

CONTENTS

1 | **Introduction** _____ 1

2 | **Markets and Qualifications** _____ 10

3 | **Getting Organised** _____ 26

4 | **Researching your Subject** _____ 34

5 | **Articles and other Short Pieces** _____ 49

6 | **Books** _____ 64

7 | **Putting it Together** _____ 78

8 | **Revision** _____ 92

9 | **Illustrations** _____ 101

10 | **The Book Publishing Process** _____ 110

11 | **Self-publishing** _____ 123

Appendix A – My Proposal _____ 128

Appendix B – Fog Index Test _____ 136

Appendix C – Useful Addresses _____ 137

Index _____ 139

Spider diagram used for planning this book

1 | INTRODUCTION

Why write non-fiction?

Non-fiction writers are often asked this question. The answer is simple: because it pays better and because it is easier to get published.

Non-fiction pays better

The idea that fiction authors earn vast amounts of money is a fallacy. Yes, there are a few authors of popular fiction who earn serious money, but most people who write fiction just don't earn enough from it to live on. I know a lot of writers, and of the 50 or so who earn their livings from their writing, all but two write exclusively or mainly non-fiction.

You only have to look at the statistics to see that the market for fiction is minute, compared with the market for non-fiction. Taking the UK as a typical example, over 100,000 books are published each year but fewer than 5 per cent of these are new adult fiction. It's even worse in the magazine field. Only a handful publish short fiction at all and most of those are women's magazines.

Despite this dismal picture, many hopeful writers continue to produce and submit short stories; far more than will ever be published, with the inevitable result that they have created a buyers' market. Presented with an excess of supply over demand, magazine editors are able to pick and choose and pay peanuts for what they do use.

Here's the other side of the story: of those 100,000 books published each year in the UK, over 70,000 are new non-fiction books, and the UK also has something like 14,000 magazines and newspapers, all needing a constant supply of material. The rest of the world is equally supplied with magazines and newspapers looking for copy.

Because the demand for good non-fiction writing exceeds the supply, payment rates are better, even for beginners. Magazines and newspapers pay set wordage rates which have to be acceptable to the professional journalists who provide most of the copy, and book publishers pay advances at rates which equate to those magazine wordage rates. For your first fiction book you will be extremely lucky to get an advance exceeding three figures.

Ease of publication

Few beginner writers understand that the market for fiction is subject to quite fast moving fashions. 'Bodice rippers' and 'S & F' (Shopping and er – sex) gave way to 'Aga sagas', aristocratic detectives gave way to 'feisty female private investigators' or, as I write, female forensic pathologists; and the market for spy stories took a serious knock when the Soviet Union broke up. It's the same in all areas of fiction.

But there always has been, and always will be, a need for factual information. From simple educational books for young children to erudite academic discussions; from basic how-tos for hobby novices to detailed analyses of political trends; the public wants to read it and so book and periodical publishers want to publish it.

This is not to say that fashion plays no part in non-fiction publishing. Magazine editors want to keep up with current trends, and newly fashionable topics can be an excellent way for novice writers to get their first pieces published. This is how I started. I had developed an interest in side-saddle riding, and had become an expert rider and instructor just as the rest of the horse world decided it wanted to ride side-saddle. I sold a series about it to a horse magazine, whose editor told me later that, because he wanted to cover the subject, he was prepared to rewrite my material if necessary. (He didn't, and I went on to write many other articles for him on various horsy topics.) With fiction, your topic can be ultra-fashionable, but if you can't write or create a good plot, no editor will want to take you on. This means you have to prove you can write the whole thing by doing just that. With non-fiction you don't have to.

Writing to a commission

It is standard practice in non-fiction publishing to commission books from no more than a proposal and perhaps a sample chapter. This means that in return for minimal effort you get a contract and an advance payment. You don't have to write the whole book before anyone will agree to publish it.

Much the same applies to short pieces for magazines and newspapers. Instead of writing the whole piece, as you would do with a short piece of fiction, you send a one-page query letter to the editor. Unless you are known to that editor from previous work the most favourable reply will be 'OK, let me see it.' This may not be a guarantee that they'll buy your article but it's more than half-way there and you won't be wasting your time on speculative pieces.

Non-fiction is easier to write

It really is easier to write non-fiction than fiction. Contrary to the idea which I've heard expressed by beginners that fiction is easier because you can make everything up as you go along, writing fiction actually requires feats of memory and organisation to keep control of invented people, places and events. Even writers of science fiction and fantasy have to draw maps of their worlds and document their other creations so they can keep track of them.

Facts, on the other hand, are already well documented, and anyone who knows enough about a favourite subject to consider writing about it already has a head full of the basics. If you need more information, you'll already have a pretty good idea of where to find it. All that is left to do is organise it into a logical structure.

Writing non-fiction alongside fiction

Writing non-fiction does not mean you have to abandon your fiction projects. It actually enables you to make some money out of those projects before you complete them, by turning the results of your research into saleable articles or even books. As well as allowing you to cash in on your efforts, this is also the solution to a problem which afflicts many novice writers.

Because they have spent a lot of time and effort in researching the facts needed to flesh out their story, novices often feel these facts will be 'wasted' if they don't use them. They cram them all in, ending up with a story that is top-heavy with irrelevant facts which interfere with the smooth continuity of the story.

For instance, your historical novel might be set in the château at Chantilly. In the process of researching the château, you find out that the complex which was built to house the horses and hounds of the creator, Henri Duke of Bourbon, is as grandiose as the château itself. Henri was a believer in reincarnation and expected to come back as a horse. The buildings are liberally decorated with statues depicting various scenes and characters from mythology and are currently occupied by a museum of horsemanship complete with live horses.

Unless there is good reason for your historical characters to go to the stables, or to discuss the foibles of their creator, there isn't much you can do with those facts in your novel. But as non-fiction you could use them for pieces on:

- seventeenth-century stable buildings
- the importance of hunting in the life of seventeenth-century French aristocrats
- the architect and/or the sculptor and their other work
- the internal structure of the actual stables and/or kennels
- all or some of the mythological characters depicted in the statuary
- Henri, Duke of Bourbon and his belief in reincarnation
- the modern horse museum
- the stable and kennel complex as a tourist attraction
- more specific articles on each of the exhibits in the museum (farriery, horses in art, horses in the bullring, etc.)

Some of these pieces would require a little more research but you can see the possibilities. I did, when I encountered the place on holiday and I have already sold a number of articles on it.

What to write about

There is so much demand for competent writing on every topic under the sun (or beyond it, if you're into astronomy) that, whatever your subject, there is a market for it.

Obviously some topics are more acceptable to the high-paying markets, but the important thing as a novice is getting the first pieces published – getting your foot in the door. I will be coming back to this theme throughout this book, as I believe it is fundamental to becoming a successful writer.

Novices should specialise

As a beginner, it is wise to keep the focus of your work tight. It is easier to persuade editors that you know your stuff if you concentrate on one area. It also makes more sense from a research point of view. The research on Chantilly needed for all the pieces I've suggested shouldn't take much more than three or four days. The research for as many articles on unrelated topics could take as much as a day for each.

So the trick is to pick a single subject and stick with it until you are established. Then you can spread yourself out a bit, adding other subjects to your repertoire. It is best if each new subject has some connection to one of the others, thus making it a logical progression, otherwise editors will think you have a butterfly mind. The progression for me was from side-saddle to general horse riding to horse businesses to running other small businesses to aspects of big business management.

Looking for gaps in the market

No magazine editor or book publisher likes to leave gaps in their coverage, so one of the most reliable routes to publication is to look for such gaps, point them out, then offer to fill them. This is another reason why specialisation helps; without a speciality, you won't have the background knowledge to recognise a gap, let alone point out to an editor why it should be filled.

Start by thinking about the aspects of your topic you would like to know more about, then research them. If you can find out all you want to know by reading no more than two books or magazine articles, you'll have to find a new angle that hasn't been covered. If it takes more than two sources to track down the information you want, you are in a good position to persuade an editor that the whole of the topic should be covered in one place.

Developing saleable ideas

As for the new angle on existing information, there's always one if you look for it through the appropriate 'filter'. For instance, look at English historical personalities with a 'county' filter and you will find that many, who aren't necessarily known as residents of a particular county, made prolonged or regular visits there. Perhaps a famous English Civil War general from Yorkshire had a married sister in Kent, whom he visited just before the battle of Marston Moor. *Kentish Life* magazine could be interested in that.

Or maybe Fred Bloggs, famous Staffordshire treacle miner turned novelist spent several months in Hampshire at a TB sanatorium after finishing the first draft of 'How black were my mine-shafts'. *Hampshire Life*, might like that. Or Fred might have had an interest in cars, and spent the proceeds of his first successful novel on the first example of a particular sports car, visiting the factory several times to check progress on his new toy. That one would appeal to the relevant area magazine, the local newspaper of the town where the factory was situated, or a car enthusiasts' magazine. Or perhaps Fred's wife wanted him to buy a car and he refused because he didn't think it was right to burn petrol for his own pleasure – an early example of the 'green' mindset which might appeal to ecological journals.

Choosing the right editor to approach

Whether you are looking to place a book or an article, all your efforts will be wasted if you don't do the essential homework of market research. I don't just mean that effort of writing a covering letter and sending it off, I mean the effort associated with preparing an outline or, if you've been foolish enough to do it, writing the whole article or the whole book.

A slight diversion here, but one that is extremely important. Every editor in the publishing world has been bombarded with so much unsuitable material from naive beginner writers that most have a deep scorn for them. Yes, they do know that everyone starts as a beginner, but there is so much published material on how to make a professional approach to editors, that anyone who is serious about their writing ought to be able to get it right.

Some beginner writers are easily recognisable from what they submit: work which is often badly typed, on non-standard paper, and accompanied by a letter which says, 'Here is a book/article which I have written and thought you might like to publish.'

Professional writers, whom editors prefer to work with for obvious reasons, never write anything unless they are pretty sure they're going to get paid for it, and then what they write is very carefully targeted for each editor's requirements. Some naive beginners seem to work from a premise that goes, 'I'll write what I want to write, then see if I can find someone to buy it.'

Unfortunately what they want to write rarely fits any editorial target and often is so far from the mark that it is obvious the writer hasn't made the slightest effort to research the market. One publisher of my books, whose firm deals only with cookery and health, tells me that she regularly gets manuscripts of poetry, children's stories and various non-fiction subjects which they have never handled.

So, do your homework properly and make sure that the project you are offering to an editor is what they want to receive. I've covered this process fully in Chapters 4 (for articles) and 5 (for books).

And when you've found an editor who likes what you do, make sure you offer more of the same. As any salesperson knows, it's much easier to sell to an existing customer than to spend all your time looking for new customers. Selling your writing is exactly the same. Do a good job often enough and you could end up in the happy situation where editors telephone you and offer you topics to write about.

Topics to avoid

Another unfortunate trait of naive writers, is to assume that an editor who has published something on a specific topic wants another piece on that topic straightaway. Editors call this the 'little lost kitten' syndrome, because as soon as they publish a story about lost kittens, their post-bag will immediately fill with other stories about lost kittens. The thinking from the writers here is presumably, 'Oh, they like stories about little lost kittens, I'll send them mine.' This is akin to 'topping' someone else's joke at a party, and likely to be just as welcome. No editor, having once tackled lost kittens, is going to touch them again, in any form, for at least three years.

This is one of the reasons for sending a query letter. Even if you have done your homework properly and found out which is the likeliest market for your piece, you can't find out, without asking, whether they have already accepted a piece from another writer on that very topic. All ideas have their time, and whatever it was that sparked off the idea in your head will have done the same for many other people. This is often falsely given a sinister interpretation by suspicious beginners who think their idea has been stolen and passed on to someone else, when all that has happened is an accident of timing.

The other thing to avoid is the clichéd idea. These are the topics that have been done so many times that anyone who reads any given area of newspapers, magazines or books, groans when they see them again. The beginner writer who is not as well read, may not have seen them and so thinks the idea is new. Some examples are 'kitten up a tree' (a variation on 'little lost kitten'), 'wives who won't iron shirts' or 'old people who take up dangerous hobbies'.

Knowing whether an idea is a good one is something that will come to you quite quickly with experience, but if you think it might be seen as even slightly trite or maudlin, it is best to leave it alone.

Things to do

- Make a list of half a dozen subjects that interest you and about which you already know a fair amount. Pick the two which you find most interesting and consider how you would pass your knowledge and enthusiasm on to someone else. Ideally one should be something practical which you know how to do, such as house decorating or playing a card game; and the other should be more cerebral, such as the use of music in relaxation or the best eighteenth-century portrait painters. This will help you to work out which type of non-fiction you might prefer to write.

- Take a topic you've been researching for your current fiction project and consider how you could turn it into non-fiction articles, using the Chantilly examples as a guide. If you find this particularly difficult, think about the sources where you found the information – history books, guide books, specialist magazines, school or university text books, etc. Is there a cross-over of sources which you could reverse, such as something from a travel guide which might be of interest to a history magazine?

- Pick up today's newspaper and read it thoroughly. What thoughts start running through your head? Although newspaper stories themselves have a very short life, they do tend to reflect public interests which are longer lasting.

■ Turn to the financial section of the newspaper and read about the companies whose annual results are reported. Are any of them doing things which you find interesting? If so, you are almost certainly not alone in your interest and you could be on to a saleable idea.

■ Read a travel guide to a foreign country, concentrating on a few towns or cities, then consider how you would write a guide to the place where you live, angling it towards your personal interests – sports, culture, arts, religion, etc.

2 | MARKETS AND QUALIFICATIONS

The markets for your non-fiction writing

What follows is not intended to be a comprehensive listing of all the types of non-fiction books, periodicals and other markets. There are so many that I could fill a whole book if I were to cover them all comprehensively, so this is a brief overview to set you thinking along lines that will lead you to publication. The different types of subject matter are called 'genre' in the publishing world. They are in no particular order here.

Hobbies and crafts

This is a very wide category, ranging from what are known as 'how-tos', to detailed catalogues for collectors. A huge proportion of book publishers deal with this category, and there are also dozens of magazines, each concentrating on a specific topic.

To enter the hobbies field you need to be able to write instructions which allow the reader to duplicate your results, and in most cases you have to produce the article in question, either at various stages of completion to allow photographs to be taken, or in its final form with your own photographs or drawings of those stages.

Whether your topic is cross-stitch embroidery or wood-working, you are more likely to succeed with a tight focus. 'Things you can make from wood' is too wide; 'Traditional wooden toys you can make in a weekend' is more likely to appeal to both the public and commissioning editors. The best-selling books and magazines are project based; an article would concentrate on one project, while a book would need ten or twelve projects.

Books for collectors are usually written by people who own substantial collections which can be photographed, or by those who already have an extensive portfolio of photographs which can be used. It's just too time-consuming and expensive to assemble all the necessary pictures otherwise.

Fewer book publishers work in this field, and most tend to concentrate on a particular area, as do most magazines. However, there are some magazines with a more general focus who are always interested in new types of collectibles, so this would be a good place to start.

Sports

Another very wide category, with plenty of scope in both books and periodicals. Whether it's 'How to improve your game of badminton' or 'Great football personalities of the 1950s', there's a market for it. If you are able to spot a new trend just as it becomes popular you should find it easy to get published in any number of places and with luck you will become known as the expert to whom editors turn.

This happened to me with side-saddle. Over the course of 20 years, I have written:

- three books on the subject
- another book on the wider subject of riding to music (a branch of competitive dressage) which included a large section on riding side-saddle to music
- chapters on side-saddle in general books on riding and saddlery
- dozens of articles for horse magazines worldwide, from the general to the specific
- articles for general interest magazines.

My earnings from this one obscure topic are now approaching the £10,000 mark, and I am still being asked to write about it.

A comparatively new aspect of sports writing concerns sports psychology, and particularly the psychology of winning. You might like to consider that as a variation on the 'How to be a better player' theme.

In addition to writing for books and magazines devoted exclusively to sport, there is also scope for writing about specific sports for local newspapers. You're unlikely, as a beginner, to get a football or tennis slot, but a quick trawl through your local paper will soon show you which sports are covered and which are not. If you put the idea to the editor, you might be able to get a weekly column of 400 or 500 words on squash or bowling or whatever. It won't pay very much, but it's that foot in the door, and it will teach you a lot about writing tight copy.

Travel writing

This is a popular category with readers, as a quick look in any library will confirm. But look a little more closely and you will see that with the exception of a few writers like Bill Bryson, the books concern journeys to exotic or remote places, and often they are made by an unusual form of transport. Bicycling the Great Wall of China, walking across Africa, horseback across Mongolia or along the crusader route from Belgium to Jerusalem, they are all a far cry from a fortnight's holiday in Malaga.

Less esoteric travel stories can be sold to magazines, but even these have to be different. Travel writing has become as cliché-ridden as kitten stories, so if you hope to get your own travelling tales published you have either to go to slightly unusual places which can nonetheless be reached by the average holiday maker, or find an unusual angle to write about.

You might go scuba-diving in a cenote in Yucatan or take a cruise up the Amazon; or you could write up a tour of all the cigar shops in Seville, or write about a group of ladies who feed the stray cats in Venice. Anything more commonplace will come straight back with a rejection slip, as will anything that is not accompanied by good colour transparencies.

Many novice writers try to write travel pieces which end up sounding like brochures or guide-books, full of the tired superlatives that no one believes. To achieve success in this very competitive field, you need to be able to write sparkling prose that makes the reader want to go straight out to buy a ticket.

Animals and birds

This category covers pets, farm animals and wildlife, with a sideline that covers both straight and humorous stories of animal-keeping enthusiasts. There are probably as many possibilities for writing for children as for adults in this category, but the single most popular animal subject is cats.

Gardening and cookery

Although it is only recently that books and magazines have included any overlap between these two subjects, I have put them together because as categories they are alike.

Both cover wide but rigidly separated strata of social class in their readership – from these who cook fish or game in their aristocratic homes to '100 ways to serve baked beans in a bedsit'; and from upmarket garden design to downmarket instructions for growing cabbage on an allotment. And whichever social layer it is, it has its own 'inner circle' of writers into which it is very difficult to break.

In the UK, the three BBC magazines – *Good Food*, *Vegetarian Good Food* and *Gardeners World* – dominate the magazine market, selling many times more copies each month than their competitors. They are written almost entirely by people who appear on TV shows, and the same people write a very high proportion of the articles in all the other magazines. In America, it's people like life-style doyenne Martha Stewart and gardener Dick Raymond. The same applies throughout the world. The cult of personality is extremely successful and it sells a lot of magazines and books, but it makes it very difficult indeed for newcomers to get published.

The only way, unless you can write for a brief local newspaper column, is by coming up with something new and/or very specialised. It took me several years to get my first gardening book published, and I know full well that I wouldn't have done it had I not hit on an idea that was not covered in any other book. That book led to another gardening book for a different publisher who was also toying with the idea of a small cookery book. I persuaded him that I should do both but because he wasn't sure I wrote the cookery book without an advance.

Shortly after it was published the company was sold and the new owners dropped the cookery book. It earned me less than £50, but I consider it was worth the time and effort to get a cookery book on my CV, which made it much easier to get a different publisher to accept another cookery book from me. That publisher wanted me to write more books, so at last I was on my way. The lesson to be learned from this is that sometimes you have to be prepared to pay, in one way or another, to get the experience that other people will pay you for.

It would be unkind of me to let you think that writing about food or gardening is an easy field to enter. Possible, if you can come up with something new, but certainly difficult.

Health and psychology

Main-stream books on health tend to be written by doctors or other people with a medical qualification which gives them authority. Books on alternative therapies also need a writer who is a working practitioner of such a therapy. In general, the same applies to shorter pieces for periodicals.

That said, there is scope for new writers who have none of these qualification if they have personal experiences to recount. Titles such as 'How I learned to live with the lurgy' or 'Living with a chronic lurgy sufferer' are always popular.

Dieting and weight loss is much the same. You have to be extremely careful about advocating specific regimes if you do not want to be sued by readers who have tried your recommended diet/exercise programme and damaged themselves in the process, but as above you can go for the 'How I ...' angle.

There is an overlap between popular psychology and 'self-help', where a writer who does not have a formal qualification can safely advocate such ideas as 'The power of positive thinking'. If you find you have a talent for the up-beat style this writing needs, you may find a mail-order publisher a better prospect than an ordinary trade publisher (see p 68).

Religion

In today's increasingly unbelieving world there is still a big demand for writing on all aspects of religion. There is also a big demand for writing on general topics for the religious periodicals, for instance travel to sites of religious interest, such as Lourdes. Obviously it helps to be a believer, but if you are this is an excellent way to get into print.

Business, management and careers

One of the most popular non-fiction book categories, all aspects of running your own business or working in someone else's business are easily saleable topics for periodicals. If you have ever run a business, no matter how small, or worked in any reasonable size of organisation, you have all the qualifications you need to write about it.

Whether it is a re-working of a 'standard' (e.g. writing reports, re-primanding subordinates, setting up a new accounting system, getting more sales, etc.) there is a market eager for it. Like health and self-help topics, these are also in demand by mail-order publishers and are often suitable for self-publishing.

To give you an idea of what is possible, my non-writing career covered a period in the motor trade, several years in the general office of a technical college, jobs with three firms of accountants and a big wine merchant while I studied to be a company secretary; then 16 years with a financial institution, where I ended up running the litigation department. As well as doing these varied jobs, which gave me a good background in all the aspects of business management and legal topics, I attended many courses on management techniques.

All of this experience has enabled me to write:

- those books on horse businesses I mentioned in Chapter 1
- a series of three books for women who want to climb the management ladder, run their own business, and take up selling as a profession
- a book version of several Video Arts training films on dealing with difficult customers
- books on report-writing, running import/export businesses and being a consultant
- numerous articles on various topics, including project management, debt collection, getting out of debt, running a car sales business, time-management, networking for career advancement, and as co-author, a book on selling paintings and another on running a product licensing business
- when I have finished this book, I will be writing a series of books on running businesses in different countries.

Think back over your own career and I am sure you will be able to write knowledgeably about many of your experiences, as I have done.

History

Writing general history books usually requires some sort of qualification – teaching experience or a history degree. More specialised books only require that you have the relevant deep knowledge, but do need a tight focus.

One area of history which offers good opportunities to beginners is very local history - that of the town where you live. Your local paper or magazine will be receptive to pieces linking current events to earlier events, or dealing with anniversaries. One enterprising woman had a slot in our local paper for several months, explaining how various streets got their names.

And although you would have difficulty persuading a mainstream trade publisher to accept a book on your town's history, such books are always steady sellers in the town itself. This is one of the few types of book which big chains will stock from non-trade sources, so local history is a good topic for self-publishing.

The suburban town where I live is the subject of several books written and self-published by two members of the local history society. They started with a general history from earliest times to the present day, then produced another book concentrating on the war, and added others as new ideas came to them. They have not yet done one on local ghosts, but I have seen this topic covered in other towns.

The sub-topic of famous inhabitants will sell further afield, especially if members of a local family emigrated to set up family branches in other parts of the world.

Educational textbooks

Textbooks can be a rewarding field, but one which is virtually closed to any writer who does not teach the subject involved. The major exception is collaborating with a lecturer or teacher who has neither the inclination nor ability to write books on their own.

Biography

The very nature of this popular genre, that of recording the whole of the subject's life, means it is almost exclusively a book topic.

Biographies fall into five types:

- Historical personalities (i.e. those long dead), for which you need an academic qualification and a reputation as an expert on the subject.
- Recently deceased political or military subjects, for which you need an academic qualification or a reputation as a political or military commentator.
- Recently deceased subjects from the world of entertainment, sport or the arts, for which you need either a reputation as a commentator or prolonged personal acquaintance with the subject.
- Living subjects, for which you need either the skills of an investigative journalist, a very hard skin and a good libel lawyer; or the co-operation of the subject. In the latter case the book may be presented as an autobiography, with the writer 'ghosting' the subject's story. Ghost writing is covered in more detail below.
- Any of the above, written for the children's book market. They are usually published in series. You could do any of these without a formal qualification, especially if you are able to find a gap in a series, but are unlikely to be commissioned to do so if you have neither qualification nor a history of previous publication.

Information for children

Like biography, there is a minimal market for short pieces here, so it is books we are thinking about, and you will be pleased to know that it is a thriving category. Children love to collect facts, whether for a school project or just their own interest, so if you have detailed knowledge of a particular subject this could be the genre for you.

However, there are some things you should be aware of:

- Most of these books are heavily illustrated, so you must be prepared to work as part of a team with illustrators, photographers and designers as well as the series editor.
- Most of these books are published in series, so you will have to conform to the structure and all other criteria that apply to the rest of the series.

■ Each series will be aimed at a specific age band, so you will have to adapt your writing to a style and vocabulary that is suitable. This applies equally to non-series titles.

This last point is actually an advantage, since if you can adapt your style, you can write more or less the same book several times for different age groups, or even for different publishers. Each publisher will approach any given subject from a different angle. For example, volcanoes are covered in several series, including Cloverleaf's 'Repairing the damage' series, which includes books on *Pollution*, *Hurricanes & Storms*, *Fires & Floods*, *Snow, Ice & Cold*, and *Famine & Hunger*, as well as *Earthquakes and Volcanoes*; and Dorling Kindersley's 'Eyewitness' series, which includes *Rock & Mineral* and *Weather*, as well as *Volcano*.

Ghost writing and collaboration

Ghost writing

Ghost writing is the situation where a person with writing ability tells someone else's story for them, either from the subject's own notes or after a series of interviews. The subject is usually a celebrity of some sort.

Many novice writers, usually those who have yet to learn the knack of finding and developing their own ideas, think ghost writing would be an easy way to get into print. However, it is unlikely they would be given a ghost writing job, as these normally go to writers of proven ability. Both publisher and subject want to be sure that the ghost will do the job properly, and will not commission anybody without a track record.

For this sort of ghost writing, if the prospect still appeals when you do have the relevant experience, there are two methods of payment. The first is a flat fee, which may be paid in instalments during the work. The other is a share of the royalties, which should include an advance payment. Either could, if you are a skilled negotiator, also include some out-of-pocket expenses.

There is another type of ghost writing which is open to novices, and that is for private individuals who will pay you to write their story. The likeliest sources of such work are people who want to record either their own or their family's lives for the benefit of future generations. This can be very interesting work, but you would be wise to insist on a written agreement which covers such details as your access to family archives, insurance of documents lent to you, ownership of copyright and your moral right to be identified as the author, as well as how much and when you are to be paid.

It is not uncommon for the 'ghostee' to suggest that your remuneration should be in the form of a share of what they optimistically see as a lucrative contract with a proper publisher. Although you might like your agreement to allow for a share of any royalties in such circumstances, you would be rash to take on this sort of writing work for anything other than an hourly rate or a flat fee. Nor should you let your ghostee continue to believe that publication is likely, because it rarely is.

Collaboration

This is a different situation from ghost writing. The former consists of your putting someone else's words into readable form. You may need to ask some questions to get all the information from them, but it is their story and your sole function is to write it down.

With a collaboration, your contribution will involve much more: information you have and your collaborator doesn't, research you do on your own, and probably the essential task of structuring the whole thing. If you have publication experience and your collaborator does not, it will be you who has to do the lion's share of preparing the proposal and outline, and your reputation that is on the line.

Sometimes collaboration work comes your way because a publisher knows your work and offers you the job of sorting out a project with an expert who can't write. Other times it will be something you and your collaborator have put together to offer to a publisher.

Whichever it is, like the private ghost writing situation you should draw up a formal agreement which covers who does what, and where, and when, and for how much and for what attribution; and who owns what if the collaboration should fall apart before fruition. I have heard too many horror stories about collaborations that went wrong to believe that a vague verbal agreement is sufficient.

What qualifications do you need?

As you will have seen from the foregoing, there are some types of writing for which you do need a formal qualification, but with the exception of textbooks, there are many other types of writing for which you do not.

What really matters, apart from the obvious fact that you do have to be able to write, is that you have to convince an editor that you know your topic. Like many fields of endeavour, this is more important when you are beginning than later on. Once you have had a few pieces published, any editor will accept that you can write. Beyond that, they all know that any competent writer can do sufficient research to find out what they need to know.

In most cases, then, all you have to persuade them about is that you have sufficient background knowledge to start the research and know whether what you discover is useful or not. So, for instance, having worked as a nurse for several years means you have enough basic medical knowledge to write intelligently on any health topic.

Another way to look at this is to consider how you would describe yourself on a book jacket. If you can't say 'Jane Bloggs is a doctor with an interest in double-jointed knees', maybe you could say 'Jane Bloggs comes from a family with a long history of double-jointed knees' or 'After going from doctor to doctor, searching for a cure for her son's double-jointed knees, Jane Bloggs found a Witch Doctor who solved the problem overnight by sacrificing a unicorn. Now she shares her experiences...'

The above refers to your first book or your first few short pieces. Once you've got those under your belt, it's much easier. 'Known to fans of willow-basket making for her book *Bulrushes, baskets and babies*, Jane Bloggs now turns her attention to...'

Agents

If I had an agent, you may be thinking, I wouldn't have to do any of this stuff, because they would do it for me. Alas, it doesn't work that way and the idea that it does is another piece of beginners' optimism.

What do agents do?

Agents sell writers' work to publishers. This is their main function – to take a saleable (note that word 'saleable') piece of writing, and using their professional knowledge of the publishing business, find an appropriate publisher to buy it, making the best possible deal for the author in the process. Some agents also handle sales of associated rights – merchandising, television, film and so on; others call in specialist associates to handle these aspects.

Their reward is commission on the money their authors earn. This commission varies, depending on the type of rights involved, but from 10 per cent to 20 per cent is the norm (plus VAT or GST, of course). The contracts they negotiate for you will stipulate that all money goes straight to them from the publishers; they keep their bit and pass the rest on to you. This applies to on-going royalties as well as advances.

The agent works for you, not the publisher. They do not, as many novice writers optimistically believe, visit all the publishers to see what books the publishers want, then find a writer to do each book. Your agent is not there to find work for you, although occasionally it does happen that a publisher will say to an agent, 'You don't happen to know anyone who could do us a book on so-and-so, do you?'

In general, literary agents are only interested in handling books. Unless you rise to the stage of earning four-figure sums for each article you write, there just isn't the money in them to make it worth the agent's while, and even then, most would only consider it if they were already handling your books.

What agents do not do is give free advice on how to write a publishable book or polish a book to the publishable stage. Their function is not that of a writing tutor or an editor and, quite reasonably, they are unwilling to do any work at all for someone who is not their client and thus will not earn them any money. Some agents have grown so exasperated by the vast number of unsuitable manuscripts they receive from hopefuls that they charge a reading fee or insist that they will only consider an outline and sample chapter in the first instance.

Do you need an agent?

This depends partly on the sort of books you will be writing and partly on your own commercial acumen and willingness to promote yourself and haggle over money.

If all you see yourself writing is articles or other short pieces for newspapers and magazines, you don't have the option, as no agent will take you on. You're going to have to do it yourself, and you may well find, by the time you do get around to writing a book, that you are happy to negotiate for yourself.

If, when you do write a book, it is of a type which will only ever sell in your own country, you don't really need an agent anyway. There isn't anything too desperately complicated to haggle over. If you have basic business sense, you should be able to understand the contract and deal with it yourself, with, perhaps, the assistance of the Society of Authors in the UK, or your local equivalent writers' organisation, who will check it for you.

It is the book which will sell worldwide, go into paperback and onto CD-ROM, or even move on to a TV series or video, that needs an agent to understand all the wrinkles and get you the best deal. If you are a really astute business-person and know your way around the publishing world, you could still do it yourself if you wanted to.

Other than these considerations, it is a matter of money. Can you negotiate a better deal for yourself in less than 10 per cent of your working time? If you can, why pay someone else to do it for you? Or would using an agent mean better deals for you than you can get for yourself? The calculation is a simple one – would you rather have 90 per cent (or even only 85 per cent) of lots of money, or a full 100 per cent of a little money?

However, having an agent will not necessarily increase your chances of getting published. It may be the case in America that some publishers will not even look at books that don't come from agents, but that does not apply in most other countries, where publishers are perfectly happy to consider submissions that come direct from writers. If your idea is a good one and your writing is competent, you don't need an agent to find it a home.

Choosing an agent

This is a bit like choosing a publisher for your book. You have to find an agent who handles the sort of book you intend to write. They don't all handle non-fiction, and those that do don't necessarily handle all types of non-fiction. It makes sense to pick an agent who specialises in your sort of book, because they will know which publishers are the best to approach and will have the ear of those publishers.

You also need an agent you can get on with, and whose operating style suits you. Some will give you regular progress reports, while others will not contact you at all unless they have something solid to talk about. Some will be happy to tell you all about developments in the publishing world in general, while others will think that shouldn't concern you. This is going to be a long-term relationship, so if you are not going to drive each other to distraction you have to check each other out fairly carefully.

Start by looking at the list of agents in your local writer's market guidebook. Pick out some likely ones and write a simple one-page query letter which gives some details of your book and asks if this is the sort of thing they handle. If they say yes and you like the look of them, you can move on to the next step of sending a proposal, outline, and sample chapter.

Assuming that they can see the possibility of selling the idea, you can move on to a meeting to get to know each other better. At that stage you can ask about the agency itself as well as what they intend to do with your book.

Don't forget that this is a two-way process and don't be too surprised if they decline to take you on. The most likely reason for this is that they just don't think you will earn enough to make it worth their while to tout your idea around the industry. For this reason, it might be better, with your first book, for you to do the initial task of finding a willing publisher, then ask an agent if they will take over the negotiations for you.

Other markets for your writing

Book publishers, magazines and newspapers are not the only paying outlets available for non-fiction writing. Businesses, educational establishments, local and national government organisations and many other private bodies often have a need for a competent writer. Here are some possibilities:

■ Businesses and other organisations need brochures, sets of standard letters, the company history, training manuals and technical manuals for their products. You need technical expertise for the latter, but it is very lucrative.

- Universities and colleges also need brochures, procedure manuals, histories and standard letters. Many are now offering 'distance learning' and need writers to turn lecture content into correspondence course material. A friend of mine has just spent two years working almost full-time for one college on this task.
- Private organisations, such as golf clubs or tourist attractions, often want brochures and brief histories. Many of them also send out newsletters, or would do so if someone was available to write them.
- Many of these organisations issue, or would like to issue, magazines to their staff, pensioners and members.

Few of these jobs are advertised and many may not have been considered until your letter and brochure arrive. You will need to spend some time in the library seeking appropriate targets for these brochures and letters, and you will have to work out an hourly rate for your services, because charging for your time rather than a wordage rate is not only the most sensible course, it is also a concept with which your clients will be familiar.

The Internet

We've been hearing an awful lot about the 'Information Superhighway' and how it is going to take over the whole world of communication and entertainment. It is, as I write this, still too early to tell if this is over-optimistic hype or an accurate prediction.

The problem, from a writer's point of view, is that most of the people who 'surf the net' think that information should be free. At the best they just won't pick up information if they have to pay for it, at the worst they pick it up and put it somewhere where everyone else can get it free. The whole thing is very difficult to police, so my feeling is that individual writers will find it difficult to sell their work direct to end-users.

However, many commercial organisations are setting up web-sites and because they want users to linger on their sites, they are looking for ways to interest them. I know of a cookery writer who has sold recipes to one of these organisations for this purpose and my grapevine tells me there are other such possibilities.

To find these opportunities you need to make contact with the people who help organisations set up their web-sites. You will find these people advertising in computer magazines and on the Internet itself.

Other than that, you might find some work by checking the forums on your service provider. In the three years I've been on-line I've seen quite a few 'job ads' for freelances, but most have been for people who write about computers and/or software. I've had very little paid work from this source. Maybe there will be more to come, but I'm not banking on it.

Things to do

- See what magazines are currently available under your chosen subject area. Consider which examples you might buy yourself and analyse what it is about them that you like. Then look closely at the other examples and work out why you find them less enticing. This will give you a better feel for the market than just reading the ones you do like.

- Buy a selection of magazines for deeper analysis at home. Go through each and make notes on the length and style of each article. Are they all aimed at readers with the same depth of knowledge? Where lengths are widely varied, what is the difference in content – complexity of subject or depth of discussion/instructions?

- Do the same exercise with a selection of books, analysing their content and structure.

- Write a 100-word blurb on your qualifications for writing on your chosen subject, modelling it on existing book jackets.

- Condense your blurb into a couple of brief sentences to include in query letters to magazine editors. You should end up with no more than 30 words, ideally less.

3 | GETTING ORGANISED

While I appreciate that everyone reading this book doesn't intend to make their living from writing non-fiction, as I do, the best advice I can give to any writer is to organise themselves as though it were their job. Even if you only write one short article a month, you are unlikely to get it published unless you present it, and yourself, professionally.

Remember always that editors want to work with people who don't cause hassle, rather than those who send in badly typed scripts that are hard to read, inadequately researched pieces that will draw complaints from readers, or badly written stuff that has to be edited before it can be used. On the whole, they would rather use reliable, experienced writers than take chances on amateurish newcomers. And they tend to judge writers by the look of what arrives in the post.

So you need to equip yourself with all the stuff that any businessperson has – letterheads, business cards or brochures, communication devices, a method of producing good quality scripts, an accounting and filing system, and somewhere to keep it all. If the way I've put that terrifies you, relax and read on. We're not talking about an enormous dedicated room for an office and lots of expensive equipment. You've probably got most of it already and you don't have to spend a fortune on the rest.

Stationery

The first thing you need is a method of convincing editors that you are a competent and experienced writer. The easiest way to do this is with printed letterheads that say 'John Bloggs – Writer'. They must look professional, so you will need to get a good original. Copy shops will prepare this, or if you know someone with a computer they could do it for you at a fraction of the cost. Once you have the original, the copy shop will run off however many you want.

Of course, if you have your own computer with a good word processing program and a good printer, you don't need to have letterheads printed at all. You just keep the basic letterhead as a correspondence document and call it up whenever you want to send a letter.

Then you need either a brochure or a CV, listing your qualifications and writing credits. The more writing credits you have, the less you need to say about your other experience. Some writers combine this with their letterhead, listing the credits down one margin of the paper ('Contributor to ..., author of ...'), others have it on a separate piece of paper. A few have more elaborate brochures printed on card.

I have a brochure which consists of one sheet of good quality A4 paper, folded in half top to bottom then in half again to make a little booklet. It involves a little juggling to get the paper in the printer the right way around for each bit, but that is minor aggravation. On the front, it says 'Janet Macdonald, Freelance Writer and Editor', with my address, phone number and email address. On the inside it says again my name and occupation, then 'Specialist in non-fiction 'How-Tos'', then after a gap, it says 'Author of: 11 books on business and career management, 3 books on gardening', and so on, listing how many books I've written in each category, then it lists some of my editing experience. Open it again, and on the inner surface it lists all the books I've written, under the various categories, with the publisher and date of publication. Finally, on the back it quotes some of the nice things editors have said to me about my work, for instance, 'I wish all my writers were as competent as you.'

Whatever you use as a brochure or CV, get the artwork done as above. There is a slight snag here. It needs to look professional, but it also needs to be up to date, which means the computer option is best. If you have your own computer, you can add each new item to it, delete the less impressive items as they become superseded and re-order them according to the piece of writing you are offering.

I do all this as a matter of course. If I am suggesting a book on a business topic, it would be silly to send a list of my publications with the business books buried in between the books on horses and gardening. So whatever the topic, if I've done anything like it before, it gets moved to the top of the list and the category heading gets underlined.

Do you need business cards? That depends on the type of writing you are doing. Some authors attach one to their brochure/CV when they submit ideas to editors, some don't. If you get all your information from libraries and never have to interview people, you probably don't need them. I didn't bother with cards until I started interviewing people in France and other European countries where they are a lot more formal. When I go to book fairs and other places where I might meet publishers I carry those brochures, as I feel it is important for such people to understand straight away how many books I've written.

If you do feel you should have business cards, you then have to decide how to describe yourself. Mine say 'Freelance Writer and Editor'. Yours could say 'Writer' or 'Author' with or without the 'Freelance'. Other possibilities are 'Journalist' or 'Photojournalist', or even 'Wordsmith' if you must.

The cheapest and quickest way to get business cards is to use the do-it-yourself card printing machines in large stationery suppliers or on mainline stations.

Other than these items, you need good quality white A4 paper for your scripts and good quality envelopes.

You should send scripts in A4 envelopes and letters in smaller envelopes, but always use business-sized envelopes, never the smaller ones sold for personal letters. Using coloured paper, cheap thin paper, cheap envelopes, or worst of all, non business-type stationery, instantly marks you as an amateurish beginner and most editors won't even bother to read what you've sent.

Sounds unjust, doesn't it? But it's a fact of writing life, and I've seen it myself from the editorial side. On two separate occasions I have had editing jobs where the first task was to sort through the responses to an advertisement in the media section of a national newspaper, to find suitable writers to commission. On each occasion, there were over 1,000 replies, and without exception, the ones that looked amateurish at first glance proved to be amateurish when I actually read them.

Communication devices

What I mean by this term is telephones, answering machines, faxes and modems for email.

Although you should never use it for your first contact with a new editor, you need a telephone so people can reach you, and also to help you with your research. You probably don't need a mobile phone: an answering machine is more valuable so people can leave messages. Editors looking for someone to do a job won't mind waiting a few hours for you to ring back, but they'll soon find someone else to ring if they don't get any response from your number.

A fax isn't essential but it is useful if you write a lot of articles with tight deadlines. If you fax it, it gets there immediately; if you post it, it might get there tomorrow if your timing is right and you live near a main post office. And while it is an absolute no-no to telephone editors you don't know, it is OK to fax them, especially if you have spotted a red-hot topical story. The point is that you might sound convincing on the phone, but it doesn't prove that you can write. A properly composed fax does.

There are three types of fax machine: the cheapish sort that uses costly special paper (which fades quickly), the expensive sort that uses plain paper, and the sort that is built into your computer. With the latter you don't have to print the faxes you receive unless you want to, and then you do it with your computer printer. To send a fax, you just produce a document as usual, then tell the machine to fax it instead of print it.

If you do have your fax in your computer, you will already have the modem which will let you send and receive email and get onto the Internet. More and more publishers and periodicals have email now, and some even like you to send your work in that way. To use this facility, you have to join a 'service provider' such as Compuserve or Demon. The main providers all advertise in the computer magazines and will send you everything you need instantly.

Typewriter, dedicated word processor or computer

Unless you are a good enough typist to produce perfect clean copy, with no typos or corrections, you should be using a dedicated word processor or computer. The days when editors were happy to accept irregularly typed scripts with correction fluid or manual corrections are long gone. A few, in the smaller publishing houses or obscure periodicals will still tolerate this, but most just consign it to the bin immediately.

If you can't afford a computer just yet, you can get cheap dedicated word processors which produce even print and let you check each line before they print it. But they do not check the spelling for you, nor do they let you save what you have written onto a disk. For that, you need a more expensive machine, which will cost almost as much as a real computer.

You will have gathered by now that I think you should get a proper computer, by which I mean either an IBM compatible or a Mac. The other, cheaper, beasts really aren't adequate: they won't produce a disk which will be acceptable to your publishers. Almost everybody wants you to send your work in on a disk these days. If you can't, they have to pay someone else to key it, and that is one of those hassles they'd rather do without.

With your computer you will need a good quality printer. Dot matrix will not do. It produces a faint result which strains the reader's eyes and some publishers will not accept work produced on them. Laser printers are perfectly affordable now, so it is worth while investing in one.

With your computer you will need a word processing program, and it is sensible to choose something which is compatible with other programs. Wordperfect, Lotus AmiPro or Microsoft Word are the commonest, and all of them have facilities that are practically the same as DTP (Desk Top Publishing).

As well as doing the various things I've already mentioned, these programs will allow you to edit your work at the press of a key or click of a mouse, automatically put numbers and headings on each page, check your spelling (which also points out most typos) and give you an accurate word count.

Convinced? You should be: no professional writer uses anything else. Although, obviously, buying a computer is a major expense, look at it this way: the machine, printer, and programs should last at least five years without needing to be replaced. If you divide the purchase cost by five, you're looking at an annual amount of money which you can earn by selling not much more than 2,000 words.

Accounting systems

You can, if you wish, keep track of the money you spend and earn with a computer program. You don't really need one though. A bound notebook will serve just as well. As long as you list everything you pay for as well as everything you earn, and keep all your receipts, you'll be able to settle any arguments with the taxman.

You could do your accounts and tax return yourself, but it doesn't cost that much to use an accountant. I have accountancy training, but I prefer to use an accountant, partly because the time-cost is less for him to do it than for me to waste writing time on it, and partly because I like to have a professional buffer between me and the taxman.

An accountant will be able to tell you which items of expenditure are allowable as business expenses. For all businesses these are fairly standard: professional fees, stationery, telephone, office equipment and so on. As a writer, you can add any costs of researching for information; the cost of books and magazines, travel, entry fees to museums, cassettes for your recorder, even ingredients for recipe testing if you are a cookery writer. When I was writing a lot for horsy magazines, I claimed a proportion of the costs of keeping my horse.

Keeping track of submissions

If you write a lot of articles or other short pieces, you will need some way of keeping track of them, whether they are finished pieces or query letters with ideas. Some people use a notebook, others operate a simple bring forward system, with copies in a folder or a concertina file with numbered segments.

Your 'office'

The ultimate luxury, for most writers, would be to have a room which they could designate as their office, secure in the knowledge that it wasn't ever going to be used for anything else. The more books and files you accumulate, the more space you need, and if like me, you work on several projects at once, you need them all to be accessible.

For most people, especially those who write in their spare time, the reality is that you have to share the computer with the rest of the family and the only 'office' you have is a corner of the dining table or the dressing table in your bedroom. The problem with this is that you have to get everything out each time you write and put it away again afterwards. Turn this irritation into a little ritual of getting everything out and arranging it in your preferred order – a piece of mental discipline which will put you in the mood to write.

Storing information

The most important type of information for a non-fiction writer is their research, and there isn't a lot of point in gathering information if you can't find it again when you need it. If you're going to take your non-fiction writing seriously, you'll want to find it again and again when you write about the same topic from different angles for different markets. So it makes sense to organise a system before you collect so much material that you can't face re-organising it.

Obviously, the format of the information will influence the type of storage, but you won't go far wrong with cardboard boxes and used envelopes. These will hold hand-written notes, periodical cuttings, photographs, letters and various other documents.

I use A4 size envelopes and the boxes which come packed with five reams of A4 paper. I stand the envelopes up in the boxes and write a heading across the top so I can flip through quickly to find what I want. What I keep in these boxes and envelopes is material relating to a specific job for as long as the job takes; or stuff relating to a specific topic which is too bulky to fit into my long-term filing system. An alternative to this costless system is rigid box-files and ring binders. I do use these occasionally, but I prefer to use clear plastic 'pockets' with ring holes rather than punching holes in the paper.

If you have room for a filing cabinet you can move on to whichever of the many available filing systems appeals to you. I have some two-drawer filing cabinets which I bought second-hand many years ago. A large piece of kitchen worktop rests on them to form my desk, and I keep correspondence and accounts papers in them.

The final method of storing hard-copy information is on record cards. They come in various sizes, but the most useful is probably 5″ by 3″ (12.5cm by 7.5cm). Quite apart from the fact that you can carry these cards in a handbag, briefcase or jacket pocket, the real advantage is that because they are all the same size, you can sort and resort them quickly and easily into whatever order you want.

They are my preferred method of storing not only notes from various sources but also recipes and any odd thoughts that occur to me. I have little stashes of them all over the house – in the office, sitting-room, bedroom; in my handbag and briefcase and in the glove pocket of the car. I was lucky enough some years ago to be on the spot when our branch library changed to a computer system and got rid of their card cabinets; for £30 I got a beautiful oak cabinet with 30 drawers, each of which can hold 1000 cards. Before that I had several purpose-made boxes which came from office supply shops.

For the computer literate there is database software. You do need to spend some time learning how to use this but once you have mastered the programs they allow you to pull out specified batches of information very quickly. The main problem with most of these programs is that you have to decide in advance exactly what sort of information you want and how to arrange it, as it has to be entered into a framework if the sort and select routines are to work properly.

However, there is one database program called 'askSam' which works on a much less structured basis. Unlike most databases, a document can be as long as you like and in any form you like. If you want to add some field markers afterwards you can, and you can ask it to search any given file (or all of them at once) for a specified word, collection of words, or phrases. It is very flexible and I use it in preference to the other databases I have available.

What it all boils down to is that there are many methods of storing information, from the costless to the expensive. You can use whichever suits you and the type of information you collect, or if necessary, all of them.

4 | RESEARCHING YOUR SUBJECT

One of the commonest causes of rejection of articles by magazine editors is shallowness. Inadequate research, or no research at all, means that although the writer may have had an excellent idea, the end product lacks depth and thus interest. You have to be seriously witty to base a writing career on superficialities, and there are few openings for witty chat pieces, so for most of us it is essential to research.

What a delightful way to earn some money, anyway. By writing non-fiction you can actually get paid for finding out about things that interest you and telling other people about them. It's not even as though you have to know everything there is to know about the subject before you start. You just need enough knowledge to recognise a saleable idea; the rest you can find out when someone has agreed to pay you for it.

Indeed, for many sorts of writing, especially anything that comes under the 'How-to' heading, it is actually best if you don't know very much at the beginning. The problem with experts is that they are often so familiar with the basics of their subject that they forget that other people don't know these basics, and fail to mention them. I once picked up a book which was meant to teach beginners how to play backgammon. The book started, 'Lay out the pieces on the board...' and went on without any instructions on how to do this, and no picture of the board or the pieces.

As a comparative newcomer to a topic it is much easier to remember all the things you wanted to know when you started, and to work out a logical route for other beginners to follow. The only time when you can't work out your own route is when you are writing for young children. In this case your first piece of research has to be how the subject is taught in schools, so you can do it in that order.

Setting up a research system

There are many ways to research for the facts you need, from using libraries or the Internet to conducting interviews; but before we look at these, I must stress the importance of having a proper system of recording and storing what you find out.

Recording information

The most important thing about researching for non-fiction writing is to mark each piece of information with its source and with the date when you acquired it. 'Source' in this context means as many of the following as are applicable:

- Where you found it. This might be a newspaper or magazine, a book, scientific paper, archive, private collection of documents or a conversation or interview.
- The full title of published documents. This should include the titles of the document or book, its publication date, the publisher, copyright owner and International Standard Book Number (ISBN).
- The full title of the author/s. This should include job titles, hereditary or awarded titles, and where relevant, family details and connections (e.g. Lady Lavinia Thingy, third daughter of the 7th Duke of Whatsit and his second wife Hermione Richgirl) and any honours or decorations.
- When it was written or said.

To record these details, you might like to adopt the system I use with record cards. I use white cards for the information itself and blue cards to record the source. (There is no significance in this colour, it just happened to be what was most easily available.) If there are only a couple of cards from each source, I put the source information on the white card.

Each blue card has a unique number, in a simple sequence which started 20 years ago with 1 and is now approaching 700. I don't differentiate between subjects. Each new source, regardless of the topic, just takes the next number in the sequence.

So, I end up with one blue card with its own number in the top right-hand corner. That same number goes on each white card from that source, again on the top right-hand corner, and the page number from the source goes on the top left-hand corner. Each white card has a topic indication written along the top, for ease of sorting.

All the blue cards are kept in one drawer, in number order, and I also have their details and an indication of the content of the white cards on my database. The white cards also go in drawers, in that source-number order, with pink cards (again, no significance in this colour) between each sequential number, every ten numbers separated by a taller card.

The reason you need all this source information is three-fold. Firstly, you may need to quote your sources in a bibliography or acknowledgements section, or if someone queries your information. Secondly, you may need to obtain permission to quote long pieces of information, and, in any case, quotes must be attributed. Thirdly, you need to know how old the information is to be able to judge its value.

This latter consideration doesn't always apply. Some facts are immutable and many opinions retain their value, no matter how old they may be. Others are superseded as science and technology advance, and some may take on a different interpretation in the light of recent discoveries.

Check and double check

If you do not want to make a fool of yourself, you must check everything you find. The main reason for checking is as above. Things change: scientists find another element or another planet orbiting the sun; new evidence comes to light to show that some historical character was a bastard (in either meaning of that word), sports people set new records, political boundaries move, etc.

The other main reason for double-checking is that unless you can find several references to something, you may be in danger of infringing copyright. More on this below.

The final reason for double-checking everything you can is that the first reference you find to something may be just plain wrong. Actually, so may others if you're dealing with a sequence of writers who've all copied a 'fact' from each other. This does happen, sometimes from something as silly as a misprint (remember the silly business about the iron content of spinach, perpetuated for years after someone put the decimal point in the wrong place?) and sometimes because the originator made a false assumption.

I heard a nice example of this at a writer's circle meeting. Someone had written an article about owls, and blithely referred to the two tufts of feathers on top of a barn owl's head as 'ears', which they are not. The true ears are on the owl's face, one above the eyes and the other down near its beak. Of course, a reader who knew better wrote to the editor and bang went that writer's credibility.

Whichever it is, the only safe way is to track the item back to a reliable and knowledgeable source or to the original document.

Copyright, plagiarism and quotations

Copyright

The law of copyright is governed by Acts of Parliament or Congress. These Acts tend to be very complex. As a writer there are several things you should know:

- Copyright is a right of ownership of a property. In the case of a writer, this means a form of words. If you are the first person who ever wrote, 'The black cat sits neatly on the mat' you own the copyright in those words. If I use exactly those words without your permission, I infringe your copyright.

- There is no copyright in ideas. If I write, 'The mat has a black cat sitting neatly on it', I have not infringed your copyright, and indeed, I have created my own copyright in this second form of words. You cannot use them without my permission.

- There is no copyright in generally accepted facts. If you write, 'Cats often sit on mats' I can use the same words because it is a fact and most people are aware of it. However, this does apply only to generally accepted and generally known facts. If the animal in question is not a domestic cat, but the rare Lesser Green Spotted Mongolian Tree Tiger, and the only mention of it is in your book *Searching for the Green Tiger*, in which you have reported that the beast has 27 green spots on each paw, 3 on each ear and 12 on each flank, and that it lives on a diet of rice and peas which it steals from goat-herders' yurts at midnight, and I then state the same facts in my own book on Mongolian wildlife, I would have infringed your copyright. A judge has said that when a degree of 'skill, judgement and labour' has gone into the selection and presentation of facts, they can be protected by copyright.

■ In Europe, you don't have to do anything to make your words copyright other than write (or type) them. As soon as you do this, the copyright is created. You don't have to register it anywhere, or do anything else. If you are really paranoid about other people 'stealing your words', you can put a copy of your work in an envelope, seal it, sign your name across the seal and post it to yourself to get a date-stamp on it and store the unopened envelope away in case of need. I have yet to meet a professional writer who doesn't think this performance is extremely childish. In America and some other countries, you do have to register your copyright. Details of how to do this can be found in your local writer's market guide, or from your local writer's society.

■ Having created copyright by writing something, it belongs to you unless you dispose of it for all of your lifetime and the next 70 years. After that 70 years, it becomes public property and anyone can copy it if they want to. This means that you can, without any problem, quote great chunks of Jane Austen but you mustn't quote Tom Clancy without permission.

■ Because copyright in a set of words constitutes property, you can sell it, give it away, or leave it to someone in your will. You can also pass on certain aspects of it, such as the right to publish it in a specific country or to publish it in hardback book form (but not in paperback, or on CD-ROM or broadcast on the radio). This is why you may need an agent to negotiate a book contract, as you may get better terms by selling some rights to a different publisher. Some aspects of this relate to periodicals, and I will go into them in Chapter 5. There are also some book situations, especially those where you work for a flat fee rather than a royalty, where the publisher takes the copyright in return for the fee.

■ You have a moral right to be identified as the writer of your work. This means that the work cannot be published under someone else's name, or even without your name. Unlike copyright, you have to formally claim ('assert') this right. Most writers put something like this on the title page of their manuscripts: 'Jane Bloggs has asserted her right to be identified as the author of this work pursuant to section 77 of The Copyright, Designs and Patents Act 1988.

■ Copyright also exists in works of art, which includes photographs as well as drawings and paintings. You need permission to reproduce illustrative material.

Plagiarism

Plagiarism is the act of copying someone else's work and pretending it is yours. It can cover not just chunks of copyrighted words, but also the structure of a book. There have been a couple of recent court cases where it was claimed that the plot and characters of one person's book were copied by another person. In a non-fiction context the way the book is structured would take the place of the plot and such details as examples or quotations would take the place of the characters.

There is a cynical view that says 'copying from one book is plagiarism, copying from several is research'. As we have seen above, generally accepted facts, i.e. those which you have found in several sources, are considered to be public property ('in the public domain'), but this does not mean that it is ethical to state these facts using the exact words from the source.

Some writers feel that paraphrasing is acceptable as long as you don't use the same paragraph and sentence order. Others don't.

What I think is this: if you can't manage to state facts lucidly in your own words, you haven't absorbed them sufficiently to understand your subject. You should go back to researching until you do reach that level of understanding.

So, no ethical writer is going to deliberately plagiarise another writer, but there is always a danger of your doing it unintentionally, especially if you have made research notes by paraphrasing what you read. What happens here is that when you come to use your notes you tend to paraphrase again from what your notes say and without your being aware of it, your brain puts it back into the original form of words.

For this reason, and also for the lesser reason that you may want to quote the original, any notes you take from another book, periodical or work should clearly show what is a direct quote and what is paraphrased. You can either use quotation marks for quotations and none for paraphrasing, or use some other method to differentiate.

This is what I do: I take notes only onto those white index cards. If a white card has a source number on it, everything on it is verbatim unless it is in square brackets, thus [ ]. I do not use quotation marks unless the writer uses them to quote someone else. If I omit part of a sentence, I use three dashes, to differentiate from the three dots which the source might use to indicate an omission.

What goes inside those square brackets is either paraphrasing, or my own comments on the rest, in which case I add my initials. If I want to check something, or what I have read sparks off a tangential thought, I write myself a note on a separate card and clip the two cards together until I can follow up the second card.

If the white card does not bear a source number, or other details of a source, I know that the words on it are my own, even though they are not in square brackets.

Quotations

For various reasons you may want to use a quotation. In informal writing it may be that someone has written something that makes exactly the point you want to. In more formal types of writing it demonstrates that you have done your homework properly, and in academic writing it is standard practice to quote authorities throughout your text.

Theoretically, under the strict law of copyright, you should obtain permission to quote any material. In practice, the doctrine of 'fair dealing' allows you to use short quotes. This was originally meant to be for criticism or review but it is also taken to mean other quotations. The UK Society of Authors' guidelines recommend using:

■ no more than 400 words for a single prose quotation
■ no more than 800 words in total for a series of quotations from one work, with no more than 300 words in each individual quote

■ no more than 40 lines or a quarter of a whole poem, whichever is the lesser.

If you stick to these limits, you are unlikely to have to pay a fee or need express permission. The major exception to this is work used in anthologies, when you must have permission for any quotations.

Be warned that it is unwise to attempt to use quotations from, or the titles of, song lyrics without permission. Song-writers and music companies take their copyright seriously and can get very nasty about infringements.

If you find you want to use a lot of quotations in your writing, the way to tackle the permissions is to write a standard letter to the publisher which explains who you are, where you intend to use the quotation, the source of the quotation (e.g. book title, date of publication, etc.) and then give the precise quotation you want to use. You don't have to copy the whole thing; you can say, 'on page 27, the section which begins "rhubarb rhubarb rhubarb" and ends, "custard custard custard".' Send two copies of this letter and ask them to sign the second copy and return it to you if they agree.

In situations where a fee is demanded, the amount will depend on where the article or book is going to be published, so you should check this with your publisher. You will also want to know whether your publisher will reimburse you for these fees.

Whether or not you pay for them, quotations must be accurate down to every last word. Even mis-spellings must be rendered as you found them, although you can add (sic) if you want.

When using quotations you must also say where they came from, although this need only be the name of the author and the title of the work, for instance, 'As Jane Bloggs said in her book *Who, Me? A plagiarist confesses...*'

Doing the research

The starting point for most pieces of research is usually finding out what someone else has written on the subject. Most non-fiction books give an indication of the sources used by their writer and you can then follow the trail backwards from book to book in whichever direction your brief requires.

When you have to start from scratch, nothing beats the telephone and a sequence of calls that starts with, 'Hello Fred, do you anyone who knows anything about green spotted tree tigers?' and moves on to, 'Hello, Fred suggested I ring you. My name is Jane Bloggs. I'm writing a book on Mongolian wildlife and Fred thought you might be able to help me with some information on tree tigers.' Occasionally the answer will be, 'Er – sorry, I'm writing a book on them myself.' Usually it is either, 'Sure, what do you want to know?' or 'Well, I don't know much about them, but Charlie does. Why don't you ring him?'

The only thing about these calls is that you should not leave them until the last minute. Murphy's Law says that if you wait until your deadline looms, the very expert you need will have just departed on a year-long field trip to the Inner Mongolian jungle where there is neither postal service nor telephones.

It's always better to phone than write. If you have a series of questions prepared, you'll get the answers straight away on the phone, whereas for most people, it is all too easy to put off answering a letter.

This presupposes that you know what you need to know. Although I am always prepared to throw myself on people's mercy and state that I've only just started my research and don't yet know what is really important, I am always working from some sort of outline that gives me a rough idea of where I want to go.

This also allows me to make sure that all the information on any given subject ends up in one place. It is not a good idea to repeat yourself in one article or book, so it pays to organise the results of your research into sections straight away.

Using libraries

The first rule for any writer/researcher is 'Make friends of your local librarians'. Tell them that you are a writer: most of them are there because they love books, so they are predisposed to approve of writers and to be willing to help them. All the librarians at my local branch know what I do and go out of their way to help me, no matter how obscure or eclectic my requests. As well as aiming me in the right direction in the reference section, they delve through micro-fiches and the borough computer for me, and they never complain when I take in great piles of reservation cards. Once in a blue moon I have to go to the Central Library to look at a book that can't be released from the reference section, but in general I am able to have books on a three-week loan to read at home.

In case you weren't aware of it, in most countries, the library system works like this:

- For most popular topics, such as computers, cookery or car maintenance, each borough or county will buy copies of a representative selection of books and periodicals for each branch library.
- For slightly less popular topics, representative material will be bought for one branch only, possibly 'Central Reference'.
- For more obscure material, it will be necessary to go outside your immediate area. There is a system by which all possible topics have been divided up into sections and each section 'belongs' to a particular library area. This area then buys every book that is published in your own country, and some published abroad, on that topic. Your local library just checks to see which area is the custodian of the topic you want to read then sends off a request for the book you want through the library interloan system.
- If the book you want is really obscure, or very old, your local library will have to apply to the national library (in the UK, this is the British Library at Boston Spa) for it.

One way or another, 99 per cent of the books I ask for can be obtained for me by my public library.

There are other libraries to which you should be able to obtain access. Colleges and universities will keep a much more comprehensive selection of books on the subjects they teach than you could find in any other single location. Professional organisations such as the Law Society (UK), or closed interest groups such as the Royal Horticultural Society (UK), have extensive libraries. Museums will have documents and books relating to their speciality.

Most of these libraries will only allow students or members of the organisation to borrow books, but equally most will let you have a temporary reader's pass to look at books in the library itself. If all else fails, ask if there is a way to find a professional researcher to do the research for you.

Public archives

Then there are the various public records offices such as the Patent Office where you can ask to see files (or a micro-fiche of them). Some of these have such complicated systems that it is easier, and in terms of time-cost, cheaper, to use a professional researcher.

If you do use someone else to do research for you, they will need a detailed brief on what you want. In general though, it is best to do it yourself, since you will find, as shown in the Chantilly example in Chapter 1, that what you are reading sparks off new ideas for articles or even books.

Information from businesses and other organisations

Large commercial or local and national government organisations are an excellent source of information on all sorts of topics. Some have a press officer, others use outside public relations companies and over the years I have found that without exception all are willing to help, send press packs, booklets and magazines; suggest other people who can help and often suggest things you ought to investigate that you may not have thought of yourself. Many will lend you photographs to illustrate your work. The unspoken quid pro quo is that you will give them a kindly mention.

Here are a couple of examples of help I've had:

- ■ For my book on import/export agencies, I accumulated six of those cardboard boxes full of information from the Department of Trade and Industry, various banks' export finance departments, shipping companies, insurance companies, accountants, Customs & Excise, freight forwarders, several embassies and an international inspection company.

- ■ For some articles I was planning for *FRANCE* magazine, one on apricot growing and one on roadside sculpture, I started with the French Tourist Board, who sent me some information on apricot farming and a phone number for the company who build the motorways in France. From another source I got a contact with a French jam making company. A couple of phone calls to France got me some more information in the post, and several more telephone numbers, of fruit growers and sculptors, from which I was able to arrange visits to these people where I got all the information and photographs I needed.

Some things you need to be aware of when using press officers and PR companies for information:

- If you don't tell them what you are doing, they may suspect you of working for a rival company and be reluctant to co-operate. I have never seen any reason for hiding the fact that I am writing a book or article, and always start the conversation by saying so.
- If you are not familiar with the Internet and its use, don't admit that you are on-line, or you will find that all you are given is a series of web-site addresses. There are even some organisations that don't have anything on paper, and whose press officers will suggest, when you protest that you don't have a modem, that you go to a cybercafé where someone will show you how to access the web-site while you both drink coffee.
- What you get is likely to be biased, often presenting the organisation as the leader in the field or skating over the less savoury aspects of the business.

On-line research

For those who are on-line, there are advantages in researching on the Internet, not least of which is that you can access information 24 hours a day, 7 days a week. The disadvantages are that until you have learned how to use the search systems, and where the information you want is to be found, you can spend many bewildered hours working your way through menus and waiting while the machine downloads pictures you don't want but can't get away from. You can also spend a lot of money on your searches, in telephone costs and in fees to some of the information providers.

I don't have space here to tell you how to use the Internet, and in any case things change on it very quickly. I can give you some general advice, though:

■ Make sure your search requests are as detailed as possible. If you ask for something as wide as 'gardening' your computer will still be tied up three days later. Make it 'Persian gardens – fountains' and you should get what you want in less than an hour.

■ Make use of your service provider's forums and Usenet groups. These will allow you to make contact with enthusiasts, who are usually friendly and helpful, and a good source of web-site addresses. However, do double-check what people tell you. I once asked in an 'Animals' forum if anyone knew the name of the furry things that dangle beneath a goat's chin. A kind, but misguided, American informed me that they are called 'waddles'. I thought this looked a bit odd. Then another forum member who is a renowned judge of goats said, 'No, they are "wattles".' (Say 'wattles' to yourself in an American accent and you'll see how the mistake arose.)

■ To save money, rather than wading through web-site databases while you are connected, get into the habit of downloading batches of topic titles or abstracts, then log off to go through them, before you reconnect to download exactly what you do need.

All of this will be much easier if you invest in some formal training. Alternatively, you can hire an experienced searcher to do it for you.

Interviews

Any situation where you visit someone to get information constitutes an interview, even though it may not actually be designated as such. So whether you're going to garner someone's recollections of your biography subject, or to chat to them about their business, the usual rules of interviewing apply.

Dress appropriately. You will earn the scorn of a city businessperson if you turn up in casual clothes, or a farmer if you turn up in strappy stiletto sandals. Scornful interviewees are unlikely to co-operate as fully as you'd like.

If you want to use a tape-recorder, ask if you may do so when you arrange the interview. Some people are nervous about being recorded, but most will agree if you explain that you find handwriting notes takes too long, and want to be sure you don't misquote them. Choose an inconspicuous machine, and have a tape in it ready to run at the press of a button.

Do your homework before you go so that you can ask intelligent questions and understand the answers. This will also help you to detect when you are having your leg pulled or the answers are more boast than fact. Keep your eye on the interviewee as you ask your questions; you will learn almost as much from their body language as you will from their answers.

Ask open questions such as, 'How did you feel about that?' instead of, 'I expect you felt pretty upset about that?' You may find you need to ask some tactful auxiliary questions to be sure the interviewee really means what they've said. A surprising number of people use malapropisms, and if someone says 'psychotherapy' you need to be sure they really mean that and not 'physiotherapy'.

And finally, beware of invitations to lunch. I remember reading of a young journalist who went to interview a famous author, who at the end of the interview said, 'We'll go and have some lunch, shall we?' He then gathered up his wife, children, the au pair and a couple of visiting friends and they all went to the local hostelry for a good lunch, at the end of which he left the unfortunate journalist to pay the bill as he departed with an airy, 'You're on expenses, aren't you?'

Building your own research library

All writers need a personal library of reference books. Start with a good 'concise' dictionary and a thesaurus, then as soon as you can afford them, or persuade Santa Claus to bring them, add a dictionary of quotations and a good general almanac. After that you can add some others specific to your special subjects.

I have a couple of horse encyclopaedias and some general veterinary books; field guides to birds, insects, mammals, trees, mushrooms, wild flowers and European crops; several books on commercial law, investment and taxation; a seven-language horticultural dictionary and several books on garden plants, shrubs and trees; *The Times* atlas, and many more. I add to them constantly (I could do with a bigger house) with every book that I write.

At the moment they are all real books, but I must confess to lusting after the *Oxford English Dictionary* on CD-ROM. I buy some new books at the full retail price, but as a Society of Authors' member I can get them through the member's discount scheme. I also keep an eye on our local remainder shop, any charity shops I encounter in my travels, and other second-hand book shops.

5 | ARTICLES AND OTHER SHORT PIECES

Market research

I've said this before and I will say it again, because it is fundamental. If you want to be a successful writer, you've got to study the market. Ask any experienced writer and they'll tell you the same. So, your first task is to find out what markets are available for the sort of stuff you want to write about.

Newsagents

The first place to research newspapers and magazines is where they are sold – newsagents, some bookshops, stations and large supermarkets. However, unless you go to a very large outlet, there will only be a small selection on display. You will also have to go several times during the course of a month, as magazines are published at different times during the month and they don't stay on display for long. Shelf space is too valuable for any given slot to be occupied by only one title, so the big retailers return any unsold copies after a specified number of days and use the space for something else.

Buy a copy of all the magazines that cover your topics and any newspapers that you think might be possibilities. Ideally, you should buy each magazine for several months to get a proper feel for its contents. With daily newspapers, you will need to buy every day for a couple of weeks.

To be frank, there isn't much chance of your getting work accepted by the big name glossy magazines until you have some quality credits under your belt, so you needn't buy those. You do, however, stand a good chance of getting into national daily newspapers – even *The Times* sometimes accepts stuff from absolute beginners, as long as the writing is good enough.

Other sources of magazines and newspapers

The usual advice given is to consult *The Writers' and Artists' Yearbook* or your local equivalent. There is a certain amount of useful information in these, including listings of periodicals by the type of material they use, as well as by subject specialisation. They give an indication of the type of content they use, as well as the address, phone and fax numbers of the editorial office, and who owns the magazine and how long it has been running. This is useful information because it may affect your chances of getting paid. Newly launched magazines are notorious for folding, and unless they are owned by one of the big groups, there may not be any money in the kitty at the end for paying freelance contributors. There is a moral here: don't do business with unknowns.

Unfortunately there are an awful lot of periodicals that just don't appear in these guides at all. For a comprehensive list of over 10,000 magazines and newspapers you need one of the directories which advertisers use – a press or media guide, or your local Rate and Data (see Appendix B). All of these directories are available by subscription only and they are too expensive for the average freelance writer to buy. Never mind, they will be in the central library and a couple of hours spent going through them should give you plenty to be going on with.

For all the periodicals listed in these guides (and there are many you may never have imagined, such as *The International Journal of Digital and Analog Communication Systems* or the *Journal of the British Blind and Shutter Association*) you will find some additional information:

- The circulation figures. This affects the advertising rates, and that affects the wordage rates they pay. Most journalists' unions, including the British National Union of Journalists, publish booklets for freelances which list these rates.

- The reader profile. This is usually stated by the standard socio-economic groups, but might be given in more detail. For example, one of the magazines for which I write offers readership statistics which defines the readers by gender, marital status, age, income, careers/retired, home ownership, credit card usership, and car ownership as well as main interests. This, and careful study of the advertisements in the magazine, will give you a good picture of the readers and the type of stories they like to read.

Make a note of the phone number for the advertising department of the periodicals that appeal to you, then ring them and ask for a 'media pack'. Try to avoid mentioning that you are a writer, as they may not be as keen to send you the information as they would with a potential advertiser. The media pack will tell you all the things I've listed and also include a recent copy of the periodical.

After that, if it is a periodical you feel you could write for, telephone the editorial office and ask if it is written 'in-house' (by employed staff) or if they use freelances. If they do, take the opportunity of checking the name and title of the person you should be writing to. This may be the main editor, or there may be another who is more appropriate, such as a features editor, a women's editor or a sports editor.

Don't restrict yourself, when you are looking for markets for your writing, to the obvious retail magazines which can be found in newsagents. Aside from the fact that there are comparatively few of them, they are the very ones which every other new writer approaches. You stand a better chance of publication with smaller circulation, specialist or trade magazines. You don't necessarily need to know about the particular trade to write for them, as long as you angle what you do write.

For instance, if your area of expertise is personnel management, ask yourself which aspects of this would apply to very small businesses and look for the magazines that cater for them. Take, for example, the topic of reprimanding recalcitrant staff without ruining the working relationship for ever. Dentists, vets and doctors all employ a few people as receptionists and nurses; small shop-keepers or franchise operators and many other businesses must at some time have to tell someone off and would like to read of the latest techniques for doing it. Sell a piece on this topic to any trade magazine, and while they might not want a personnel piece in every issue, there is a good chance that they will think of you when they do.

The other point about trade magazines is that the people who read them may be dentists or franchisees, but they are also human beings and have as wide a range of interests outside their jobs as anybody else. Dentists play golf, doctors drive cars, vets go on holiday and all of them have to put up with relatives at Christmas or find birthday presents for children. If you can't find a topic to write about for them you just aren't trying hard enough.

Keeping track of editors

In any type of business, and writing is no exception, the people who do best are the ones who keep up to date with developments in their industry. Take the trouble to find out what is going on: what new magazines are being launched, which are folding or being amalgamated with others, and most important of all, which editors are moving.

For this valuable information you need to read trade magazines such as *Press Gazette*, which deals mostly with newspapers and to which you have to subscribe, as well as the media section of the national daily newspapers. In both of these, look at the job advertisements. You will occasionally come across adverts seeking freelance writers (see my comments above on the number of replies these draw) but you will always see adverts for editorial jobs in magazines and newspapers.

The person who gets the job isn't going to be in place for some time – at least a month – so make a diary note to ring then and ask the switchboard if the new editor is in place yet and who it is.

New editors usually like to have a complete change of writers. This is bad news if you've been a regular contributor, but good news if you've never written for them before. If you give the new editor a week or so to settle before you send a query letter with an idea, you stand a good chance of getting a commission.

Overseas markets

Just as we like to know how foreigners live, readers in other countries want to know how we live. Whichever country you live in, there will be foreign nationals, as well as hundreds of thousands of people who started life in one country but now live in another, who like to be reminded of their old lives. There are also many who plan to visit the country from which their recent or distant ancestors came, and for whom reading about that country is part of planning their trip.

And then there are all the people whose jobs or hobbies are the same as ours, who are interested in all the things that interest us. Dentists in Australia and Sweden have to reprimand their staff too, and they also have trouble with their golf slice.

Some topics don't travel because the way things are done in one country is unique, but others do. For instance, the way British children compete on show ponies is unlike any other country, but there is only one way to ride side-saddle and I have sold articles on it to horse magazines in many countries.

A good source of general information on other countries is the government export department. Ask for the free guide on whichever country you are interested in, which will give you a good idea of what topics might be appropriate. For information on magazines published in any specific country, enquire at that country's embassy (addresses from your library).

The best way to get all the information you need about markets abroad is to join the writers forums or usenet groups on Internet service providers. If you do your bit by providing information on markets here, you will find plenty of people in other countries to do the same for you.

Newspapers

As I've mentioned above, national daily newspapers do sometimes accept work from unknown freelances. Regional dailies or evening newspapers do also, but like weekly local newspapers they cater for local people, so if you are writing on general topics you must offer a local slant.

So, if your topic is gardening, you are unlikely to succeed in placing articles in papers 300 miles away from your home. You may believe you know what will grow there and when it needs attention, but your problem is going to be convincing the editor. For this reason it is sensible to confine your efforts closer to home.

It is features we are considering here, as news items will be dealt with by staffers, so it is the features editor you should approach. Obviously, you should first have familiarised yourself with the style and content of the paper (it is amazing how many novice writers don't bother to do this, then wonder why they get rejection slips) and your suggestions should also conform to the wordage length that seem to be the norm.

When you are studying the paper, watch out for the items which are surrounded by advertisements for goods or services relating to the topics of those articles. You may be looking at 'advertorial', material put together from advertisers' handouts. You are most likely to encounter this in free newspapers, but some localised magazines do it too. It's a good cheap way to produce a magazine, but not a lot of use to a freelance writer.

Other magazines, especially those aimed at customers of a particular product (for instance many car magazines) do take pieces from freelances but are 'advertisement led'. This means that they want to be able to link your article with some advertising. For instance, an article about Venice would need to be linked to advertising from a travel agent or airline.

Syndication

To think that writing for a syndication agency would be a good way to get into print without having to do all that nasty business of selling your work is a false assumption. Leaving aside the fact that you first have to sell yourself to an agency, they only accept work that has been previously published and they won't take on anyone who can't keep them supplied with a steady flow of material. Unless you are well known to the public, agencies won't take pieces on the more obvious topics, partly because they will already have a large stock of such pieces.

This is not to say that you can't syndicate your own material, especially if it covers such timeless topics as collectibles or money. This is another situation where you need those press directories for some names and addresses, choosing papers or local magazines whose circulation areas do not overlap each other. You'll need to write a good selling letter and to enclose some samples of your work. For syndicated work that does sell, you won't get more than a fraction of the original price; but if you can sell each article several times it soon mounts up. If you work through agencies, you may find they keep half of what they collect for you.

Part-works

If you have expertise in topics covered by part-works (those one-a-week magazines which build up to an encyclopaedic book), you may be able to obtain commissions to work for them. Popular topics are various aspects of home-making (cookery, needlecrafts, DIY or gardening) but they can also cover such subjects as ponies, wild-life or steam trains.

Find the part-works in larger newsagents and look at several of them. You will find that most of them are published by the same two or three specialist publishers and it is worth ringing them to see if there are any others planned that might cover your pet subjects. For the titles that are already running, ask how many parts are planned and what their lead-time is.

Like all publications that involve colour photography, part-works are sent to the printers many weeks ahead of the publication date, and commissions are made several weeks ahead of that. So if the whole is going to be 52 parts and part 26 is on the news-stand already, you don't stand much chance of adding to it.

When you are commissioned, you will be given a very detailed brief. Don't be surprised if you find they have rewritten your contribution: many publications have a rigid house style and find it easier to get editors to rewrite everything in that style. You won't get a by-line on your piece but you should be listed in the front among other contributors. In general, this is one of those situations where you get a flat fee.

Composite book projects

When you are known for your expertise in a particular topic, you may be able to write a section on your speciality for a general book. I've done this a couple of times: once on riding side-saddle in *The Complete Book of Horses* and once on the saddles themselves in *The Country Life Book of Saddlery*. In both cases I was approached by the project editor, but if you have such expertise and can prove it either from formal qualifications or a convincingly long list of publications, there is no reason why you should not write to the commissioning editor of likely publishers to tell them of your existence.

Again, it is usually a 'flat fee buys your copyright' situation but the money should be acceptable and the exposure useful.

Fillers and other short pieces

Fillers are very short pieces, often as little as 50 words. They can be humorous, personal anecdotes, inspirational thoughts, household tips or even short quizzes. The classic filler is the sort of thing you see in *Reader's Digest* and they can be very lucrative, viewed on a wordage basis.

Editors like them because they can be used to fill awkward gaps at the ends of columns. Remember that newspapers in particular are 'made-up' to a very tight deadline and editorial copy and adverts have to be juggled to fit. If a gap opens up, no one has time to write something, they just reach for the file of fillers and slot one in.

The normal routine is to accumulate a batch of fillers (one per sheet of paper with your name and address at the bottom) then send them in. It's worth a phone call first to find out what the payment situation is: some magazines will pay you for each one as they use it, while others will be happy enough, once they know you, to buy a batch from you and use them whenever they need to.

Don't scorn writing letters to the editor. There are people who make a serious side-line of this, circulating letter topics around various periodicals and keeping meticulous records of which letter has gone where. The valuable thing about writing letters for publication is that it hones your skill at getting your point across in a short piece and it also teaches you to observe what concerns the readers of any given magazine/paper: a skill which you can then use to good effect in longer pieces. If you can't get into print any other way there is nothing wrong with a follow-up personal letter to the editor which says, 'You've published a number of my letters. Now I would like to write a longer piece for you...'

Supplying the market

Once you've found some likely periodicals or other outlets for your work, the next steps are to persuade those markets that they would like to use your work, and finally to write and send it. And you must do it in that order. Editors do not want to see articles on 'spec': they want to see ideas. If they like the ideas, then they'll ask to see the article.

Query letters

There's an old advertising adage that goes, 'You never get a second chance to make a first impression'. This means that your query letters to editors have to be perfect if they are not to go straight into the bin. That doesn't mean they have to be models of formality, but you do have to get the obvious things right, like the editor's name and gender.

The main body of the letter should ideally take one page, and it should cover no more than five things, in this order:

- The idea and why it will interest readers.
- How you will develop the idea.

- That you can supply colour transparencies or black and white photographs (assuming that you can).
- How long it will be, to the nearest 100 words (making sure this is the same as similar articles you've seen in the periodical).
- Your qualifications for writing it.

Then you say that you are enclosing some copies of your work and that you look forward to hearing from them. If you don't have any published work to show, it may help your case to give your intended opening paragraph.

That's all it needs. No return postage, no 'This is my first attempt at writing for magazines', no 'I'm sure I can do a good job of this subject', and nothing else that will mark you out as a beginner.

Why do I say you shouldn't send return postage? I never do. My experience is that I still get a reply, even if it is 'No thanks'. On the rare occasion that I don't get a reply, what have I lost? Maybe a couple of sheets of photocopies, which will cost me less than a second class stamp to replace. I've got to print another letter anyway, so there is nothing else that I can re-use. The advice that you send return postage may have been valid in the days when it was a major operation to re-type CVs and so on, but now it only takes a click of the mouse to get a clean new print.

There is no reason why you shouldn't write your query letter to several editors at once, modifying the length of the piece and how you will develop it as appropriate for each magazine. Most books on writing tell you that you shouldn't do this, which is silly. Why should you wait for each of a series of editors to say No before you move on to the next? There is very little chance that all of them will say yes if you write simultaneously, so all you've done is saved yourself a lot of time. If more than one does like your idea, you can either find out which pays best and abandon the other, or write for both, making sure that the two pieces are completely different.

There are other things to avoid when you approach an editor for the first time (or even the second or third time). The first is to offer to write a regular column for them: they just won't commit themselves to regular slots from unknown quantities and they'll think you ought to know it, which puts you straight into the naive beginner category. The second is to offer a whole list of ideas on disparate topics: this smacks of a take-over bid and they won't like that either.

When you've had a few pieces accepted, by all means suggest a three- or four- part series, if they have a history of publishing these, but otherwise, 'one at a time' is the rule.

But do keep the ideas flowing once you've had one piece accepted. Repeat business is always easier to obtain than new business, and as long as you keep up a flow of good work you'll soon get to the stage where the editor rings you to ask for something else.

Some writers make a practice of confirming, by letter, the editor's agreement to look at an article. Even if you don't do this, and it does no harm, do accompany the actual article with a letter which says, 'This is the article you asked to see on such and such a date.' If you don't do this, there is a chance that your piece will accidentally end up on the slush pile.

The final but probably most important point about sending in your article is that it should be accompanied by an invoice. Some magazines will pay you without one, but most expect you to send one. All newspapers require an invoice. Both will want to know if you are VAT/GST registered and will need a proper invoice if you are.

This raises the delicate question of how much you are going to get paid. The only way to find this out is to ask, and the way you do that depends entirely on your personality. You can either ask the bald question 'How much are you going to pay me for this?' or approach it a little more obliquely 'Oh, by the way, I assume this will be at standard union rates? Which category are you?' (This refers to the advertising rates categories related to the minimum wordage rates recommended by journalists' unions.) If you don't fancy asking the editor, talk to their secretary or the accounts department.

Submitting the finished work

When the body of your article is written and polished to the best of your ability, it's time to produce a hard copy and (if applicable) a disk. All the usual rules for typescripts still apply:

- Use only one side of the paper.
- Don't use fancy typefaces.

■ Leave wide margins on both sides, top and bottom.

■ Double space your lines and leave another double space between paragraphs.

■ Use nothing but a paperclip to hold the pages together. Number and title all the pages.

■ For newspapers, put 'more' or 'm/f' (more follows) at the bottom of every page except the last. Put 'end' at the end. Put your name, address and the title on the first page. I put these on a separate page and no one has ever complained, but my newspaper journalist friends tell me that they put it on the top half of the first page and begin the story underneath. Choose titles and sub-titles that are short and to the point. Don't be surprised if these are replaced: sub-editors often think titling is their prerogative.

Should you put 'First [Country] Serial Rights' or 'F[X]SR' on the first page? Certainly you should. It means that you are offering the periodical the right to print the article once only, in your country, which leaves you with the right to syndicate it or sell it abroad, or sell it in any other form. There has been a furore running for some time over the big periodical publishing groups' insisting that they buy 'all rights', which includes the right to publish your work in book form or on the Internet.

Professional journalists are up in arms about it. They suggest that when you get a contract note that says 'all rights' you should change this to F[X]SR. They can't take any rights from you unless you agree, but signing an unaltered contract note constitutes agreement even though the typescript says F[X]SR. Altering the contract may work, or it may result in the editor rejecting your work. I can't, I'm afraid, offer a definitive answer, but I would say this. Before you make a potentially suicidal fuss about your rights, ask yourself if it is worth it.

If you know you can syndicate your work, if you are writing pieces that can be turned into a book, or if your work is really so good and unique that you feel you could sell it again elsewhere, it is worth insisting that you retain the right to do so. But if this piece of work is just another standard piece on a common topic (for instance 'How to preserve water in a drought') or if you are a beginner and have few other writing credits to your name, my advice is to keep quiet, sign the form and accept the money.

When you're starting out as a writer, getting your work published at all is more important than sticking to this sort of principle. Come to think of it, it's actually more important than getting 'top dollar' too, or the putative glory of getting into a well-known publication, which is one of the reasons the wise beginner starts with more obscure titles. It's a simple equation: increase your chances by choosing markets where there is less competition from experienced professional journalists.

Disks

Most magazines, and some newspapers, want copy on a disk as well as on paper these days. Some even like it by email. Unless they have said otherwise, disk means a standard $3^{1}/_{2}''$ floppy disk, with an IBM compatible text format. Some may specify the word processing program they use, and if you expect to do a lot of work for them it is worth spending a couple of hundred pounds to buy a copy of it. Otherwise any program which is capable of saving to disk in ASCII is acceptable.

They will probably specify some technical or style details, for instance no underlining or leave only one space after a full stop. There should be no other files on the disk besides the work you are submitting.

Don't forget to put your name and the title on the disk label. (You'd be surprised how many people do forget this!)

Finally, don't be a cheapskate and ask for your disk to be returned. They cost so little, compared with the amount that you will be paid for what's on them, that all you'll do is put yourself in the same category as the sort of beginner who won't spend money on decent paper or a new printer ribbon.

Some magazines do send your disks back anyway. A wise person runs them through a virus checker before they do anything else with them.

More on money

Although most big publications pay a standard rate for all features, some pay what they refer to as a 'negotiable' fee. This means that if they can get away with paying less to a novice they will. Some editors will counter your query about union rates by asking if you are a member of the union, then say they don't pay those rates unless you are. It's up to you whether or not you want to work for these editors, but as a novice there isn't much you can do about it. This sort are quite capable of telling you to go elsewhere when you get more experienced and ask for more.

Perhaps a better way to deal with them (and they should be detectable by their terse manner before you get to this stage) is to ask the straight, 'How much are you going to pay ?' question, followed by, 'Is that all?' if you don't like the answer. I've found this to be surprisingly effective: most often the response is a better offer.

If you are writing anything regularly, even those weekly slots on golf or badminton for the local paper, it's worth asking for a rise every so often. Obviously you shouldn't do this too soon, but once a year is perfectly reasonable.

A concept you should be aware of is the 'kill' fee. This is the amount that you should get when a piece which has been firmly commissioned is dropped and not used. The British writers' organisations recommend 50 per cent of the agreed amount if the work has not been completed, but 100 per cent if it has. In this situation the rights revert to you, so you can offer first rights to any other publisher.

'Payment on publication' can be interpreted very widely. Given that most magazines appear on the news-stands halfway through the month before the month when they are nominally for sale (i.e. the March issue is on sale by 15 February) you might hope to get paid in February. Hope on, but don't be surprised if you are not. It could be up to two months later. At the worst, the editor will sign the invoices for March items at the end of March, then they go to the accounts department who will put them into the computer system for the next bought ledger cheque run which could be at the end of April.

The first time you get a piece accepted by a publication which is new to you, it does no harm to ring the accounts department to ask if your invoice has reached them, if it was in acceptable form, and what their policy is on the timing of payments. Then, if nothing arrives in that time-scale, you can start chasing.

The first step is to send a statement with a copy of the invoice and a note on it that says 'Due for payment now'. If this doesn't work, and a friendly phone call doesn't work, you will have to go into the standard debt collection routine: a polite 'I don't seem to have been paid' letter, followed by a 'Please pay within seven days or I shall be forced to take legal action' letter, followed by a visit to your local Small Claims Court to issue a writ.

Don't worry about this possibility. It is unlikely to happen to you if you stick to reputable publishers. It is more likely if you take on work for fringe publishers or other small businesses. With these, the best routine is to minimise your risk, by waiting until you get paid for the first piece of work before you do any more, and never letting a backlog of unpaid work build up.

For the small businesses or any other private situation where you will be spending a substantial amount of time on the work, it is wise to arrange a series of stage payments. If the job is going to take many weeks, a weekly payment is not unreasonable. Otherwise the norm is three or four payments, with the first one up front, the next one halfway through and the rest either on delivery or after final editing.

This is what I do, and I lay down my pen at each stage until the payment comes through. I prefer four payments and my standard letter of agreement allows for me to nominate an outside editor if there is any argument as to when the editing process is complete. It also says, where appropriate, that copyright does not pass until payment is received.

I also charge a 'consultancy' fee up front for looking at the job, when I have been recommended for it by a third party for whom I have previously worked. I know from experience that you can easily spend a couple of days looking through a mishmash of notes or badly written material while you work out how long the job will take. I take the view that anyone who isn't prepared to pay a reasonable fee for a professional opinion isn't going to want to pay a professional's fee for getting the job done.

How do I price the actual job? Easily enough. I know, more or less, how long it will take and I know how much I want for my time. I usually add a couple of days worth of time-cost for complications, then point out to the customer that if they want it in a hurry, it will cost them extra to disrupt my existing work schedule. I don't mind working long hours to get a rush job done, but I do expect to be compensated for the inconvenience.

Things to do

■ Take one of the article ideas you worked out for the exercises in Chapter 1, find five or six sub-topics and sort them into a logical order for an article. Write a short paragraph on each.

■ Rewrite these paragraphs to make an appropriate article for each of your two likely magazines.

■ Write a query letter for each editor and send it.

■ Look through the latest copy of your favourite magazine, and without reading the articles, list the titles that look interesting. Write an article on each topic, then read the original articles to see how that writer tackled the subject.

■ Study today's issue of two very different newspapers. Write a letter to the editor of each, in appropriate style, about an article in the paper.

■ Now draft an article on each topic for the other paper, in appropriate style and applying appropriate sentiments.

6 BOOKS

It has always been my conviction that people who insist they want to write short stories do so because they are frightened of having to produce the number of words required for a full-length book. One thousand words is difficult enough, they reason, so 100,000 must be a hundred times as difficult. The same rationale applies to non-fiction. I know many experienced journalists who are convinced they couldn't manage to write a whole book, despite the fact that they are producing between 5,000 and 10,000 words a week in short pieces.

Non-fiction books, in general, don't have to be as long as fiction. An average figure is probably 50,000, and that, even if you can only manage to produce 1,000 words a week, is less than a year's work. Of the 26 non-fiction books I've written to date, only three were over 100,000 words, and 16 were 50,000 or less.

It's achievable for anybody. And I promise you, it is easier to do your topic justice in a book-length project than in shorter form. In a book, you can say everything you need to. In a short article, you have to select which parts of the topic you can cover, then prune and prune to get your message across in the limited space.

The other thing about writing non-fiction books is that you get paid a fair chunk of the money up front, as an advance on the royalties. Whatever the amount offered, and it is usually a calculation based on the likely first year sales, the normal arrangement is for a proportion of it to be payable when you sign the contract; but whichever way it comes, you get some straight away.

So, once you have decided that you have enough material on your topic to write a book, you have to find an appropriate publisher to write it for, just as you do when you want to write a shorter piece.

Market research

I did warn you that I'd be saying this again: study your market. It's silly enough to spend time on writing 1,000 words then trying to find a buyer for them. You certainly don't want to write 50,000 words unless you are sure someone wants to buy them. So, as when writing for magazines, you need to find out who publishes the sort of thing you want to write.

Start by asking at your library for *The Bookseller* (or your local equivalent). This is a weekly UK magazine, aimed, as its title shows, at the book selling trade, but which has become very much the 'bible' of the publishing industry. Each week, as well as job adverts for editorial staff, it lists all the books that have been published during the week and it also features certain genres at regular intervals. Useful though this is, even more useful are the two bumper issues, in February and August, which cover most of the books to be published in the next six months. These are shown under genre category, with titles, publishers, and a brief description of each book. Some publishers also take advertisements in these issues, showing all their books on one or two pages. A whole year's subscription to *The Bookseller* might be more than you want to pay, but you can subscribe for these two editions only.

The next step is to go to a big bookshop and look at the books themselves. Be sure to check publication dates in the front of these books. Some of them may be reprints of older books and what you want to know is who is publishing new books on your topic now.

Some topics are sold by specialist bookshops or mail-order outlets. Although these shops tend to be in big cities, you may find it worth while making a visit. Not only will they stock all the current books on the topic (both home published and from abroad), they will have such detailed knowledge of books on their topic that they will be able to tell you what sort of demand there might be for what you are thinking of doing.

While you are looking at books, check to see what is missing. Publisher A does books on sports but doesn't seem to have any on badminton. Publisher B has several on tennis and badminton but nothing on squash. If racquet sports are your thing, there are two possibilities straight away.

Before you leave the shop, if you do not already have one, buy the latest copy of your local writer's market guide, because your next task is to telephone the publishers and ask for a copy of their catalogue. Once you have a selection of catalogues you will have a much better picture of who does what.

There is one other way to find out what publishers are doing, and that is to go to a publishers' book fair. These tend to be enormous affairs running for several days, and all local publishers (as well as a lot of others) have stands there. Wear comfortable shoes and take a stout bag to hold catalogues (I've seen people with wheeled shopping trolleys).

Collecting catalogues and asking the sales reps for the names of the relevant commissioning editors is the reason you go: these book fair stands are staffed by salespeople who are there to sell books to the trade, or to sell co-editions to other publishers. Generally they don't have the time, let alone the inclination, to talk to writers, and some of them can be quite rude if you ask about the possibilities of doing a book for them. Other than, 'May I have a catalogue please' and 'Do you know the name of the commissioning editor for your sports series?' the only thing you might say is, 'You don't seem to have a book on badminton in this series' which could get a useful response like, 'We were only remarking on that the other day. They said they'd think about doing one' in which case you'd better get your proposal in a bit quick.

Whichever way you get hold of a selection of catalogues, once you have them you will be on your way to compiling a shortlist of possible publishers. The next step is to get hold of some of their recent books to narrow the field a bit more. You can't always tell from the catalogue what the books are like, and you need to know because you are going to have to do your book more or less the same way if you want to get it published. To keep your expenses down, I suggest that you use the library reservation system rather than buy copies at this stage.

What you are looking for is the general style and structure of the books from each publisher. In series publishing you have to stick fairly rigidly to this, but even in non-series publishing your chances of getting a commission will be improved by sticking to the norm.

Remember that the object of all this is to get into print, not to reform the world. You may feel strongly that a book on racquet sports should start with detailed instructions on how to hold the racquet, not with details of the scoring system. But if there is only one publisher without a book on badminton in their sports series, and their books on tennis and squash start with scoring, then that's how you should do it.

Useful though the catalogues are, they only give you a historical picture of what any given publisher is doing. It doesn't tell you what they are thinking of doing in the future, and thus what you could offer to do for them. That information isn't generally available: it comes close to the heading of 'trade secrets', but there are a couple of ways you can get some hints.

The first is the old-fashioned method of keeping your ears to the ground: reading everything you can on the publishing industry. The primary source of this information is trade magazines, but the books sections of the national newspapers (especially the Sunday editions) are also useful for information on general trends. For more specific information, the second method is those job adverts for editorial staff, which often say something like 'as part of our planned expansion in sports books...'

Choosing the right publisher

Trade publishers

When it comes to choosing specific publishers for your book projects, the situation is exactly the same as it is with magazines: the big-name glossy publishers are unlikely to be interested in work from a novice writer, so you stand a much better chance of acceptance from a smaller publisher – and a quicker response, too. The larger the publisher, the more rigid the systems, and so the longer everything takes.

With a big publisher, your proposal starts with a commissioning editor. If they like the idea, it will go to at least one outside reader for an opinion. If the response is dubious, the proposal may go on to another reader, or you may have to rewrite it to bring it in line with that reader's suggestions. Enthusiastic responses move it on to an acquisitions committee meeting, which may take place only once a month. At best this process will take three months, at worst it can take a lot longer.

But with a smaller publisher, where the commissioning editor is likely to be one of the owners of the firm, they will either make the decision themselves or talk it over with colleagues. I don't say it will always be this quick, but I've had a decision to publish within a fortnight of submitting my proposal.

Mail-order publishers

Let me start with a brief definition of what I mean by mail-order publishers. Unlike trade publishers who sell their books through the book trade (i.e. via wholesalers to retail book shops) these publishers only sell books by mail order. If you write for them, you won't see your books in bookshops and you probably won't see them in libraries, either. Some sell straight from advertisements in magazines and newspapers, others through catalogues.

There seems to be a vague idea amongst writers that there is something unprofessional about this approach, but I can assure you that this is not the case. My experience (and I have written several books for this type of publisher) is that they are extremely professional, know exactly what they want, pay very quickly, publish very quickly indeed, and sell a lot of books. My *Gardening Tips* was commissioned in mid-May 1995, delivered mid-August 1995, the full advance cheque was paid four weeks later, the book was launched in January 1996, and 18 months later it had sold over 35,000 copies and I'd been paid the royalties for them every quarter.

There are only a few mail-order publishers who handle a range of general topics, and they seem to be majoring on self-help and health topics these days. Several more publish books on various aspects of running and managing businesses, and there are others who specialise in only one subject for special interest groups. You can only find them through their advertisements, and you can only get hold of their books by buying them, as you won't find them in libraries.

Book packagers

These are a comparatively new area of the publishing industry. They deal mainly with heavily illustrated books which have international sales potential through what are called co-editions.

What packagers do is produce a book to a stage just short of actually publishing it: they use freelance writers, photographers, illustrators, designers and editors to create a package of an idea which they then sell to publishers. Each publisher buys the right to publish an agreed number of copies of the book in their own country, and then has to do no more than sell it.

The packager will have a standard minimum number of copies which they consider makes a project viable (usually between 30,000 and 40,000 copies), but they will make up that number by selling batches of copies to several publishers. A British publisher might take 10,000, an American publisher 10,000, a German publisher 10,000 and an Italian publisher 10,000. For each book, the pictures and layout are identical and are printed in one big print-run, then the 'black' matter – the text, index and so on – is translated and printed separately for each publisher.

If you have an idea for a book which requires heavy illustration, you might find it easier to sell it to a packager than direct to a publisher. Some will offer you an outright fee for your writing, although this is more likely if they commission you to do the text for an idea that they have generated themselves. (Once you have some good credits to your name, it is worth offering your services to packagers.) Most, when it is your idea, will offer you a royalty. This won't be as much as you'd get for a straight textbook from a trade publisher, but you will get all of it for any given print run when each publisher takes delivery rather than having to wait for copies to be sold to the public.

Offering a non-fiction book to a publisher

Offering to write a book for a publisher isn't that different from offering to write an article for a magazine. The difference is the scale of the end product and the cost to the publisher of producing it, so there is also a scale difference in what you have to send to the publisher.

The whole of what you need to send is called a proposal, and it consists of these items:

- A covering letter.
- Your writing CV and a couple of examples of your work.
- The proposal itself.
- An outline (also called a synopsis) of the book.
- On request, but not before, a sample chapter.

I've listed these in this order because this is the order in which the recipient will look at and deal with them. Each document supports and enlarges on what has gone before.

You should not send a completed manuscript with your proposal. If you do, it will go onto the general slush pile and sit there until someone gets round to looking at it. This could be anything up to three months later. Worse still is to send a completed manuscript without a proposal, for that immediately marks you as an amateur, and it also leaves the sponsoring editor with the task of preparing a proposal to submit to the next acquisitions meeting.

Send in a proper proposal and it will get looked at straightaway, by an editor happy in the knowledge that they are dealing with someone who knows how publishers work.

The covering letter

As with all covering letters, this one should be brief and to the point. It should be addressed to the right person, with the name and title correctly spelled, and there must be no other spelling mistakes or typos. Would you trust the writing of a whole book to a person who can't even write a letter properly?

It should occupy no more than one sheet of paper, and consist of no more than three or four paragraphs.

- The first paragraph says that you are enclosing a proposal offering them a book on whatever, and continues with a few lines encapsulating the contents.
- The second paragraph summarises your qualifications for writing the book: umpteen years of studying or teaching the topic, or writing about it. If it applies to you, mention that you are enclosing more details of these qualifications on a separate sheet.
- If applicable, a brief mention of your other writing credits and how well they were received. Again, you can enclose more detail on a separate sheet.
- A closing paragraph which simply says that you hope your proposed book will be of interest and that you look forward to hearing from them.

This letter enables the editor to make a series of rapid decisions:

- Is this proposed book going to fit into our list and do I have a need for it?

■ Does this person have the necessary knowledge of the subject?

■ Can this person write, and will this person write the book?

As with magazine articles, if the topic you are proposing is one which the publisher is anxious to cover and you clearly know your stuff, they probably won't mind having to give your manuscript a heavy edit, although obviously they'd rather not have to. Of more concern is whether, after they've given you some money, and committed a slot in the production schedule to your book, you will actually produce it on time or at all. If you are able to show that you have been published, that worry will be immediately alleviated.

Your writing CV

This only applies if you have a lot of varied writing credits, more than can be covered in a four or five line paragraph in the covering letter. I don't mean to suggest that a lack of this sort of CV will spoil your chances, because it won't if you know your stuff. One way of giving the impression that you are a serious writer is to list work in progress as well as published work. You can list it under that heading, or do as I do, by adding the titles of commissioned books to the appropriate section of my CV with 'for [date]' instead of the published date.

But if you are in a position to quote, either in that paragraph or on your CV, something on the lines of, '"the most popular series on badminton we've ever run" – editor, *Racquet and Ball* magazine', it is obviously going to help. Photocopies of this sort of letter, or appreciative reviews, as well as of a couple of your articles, can be attached.

The proposal

This is the most important document, because it is the one that will be passed on to other people in the publishing house as well as outside readers. It will be accepted that the editor sponsoring the book is satisfied that you're competent to write it. All these others, who will include accountants, designers and marketing people, are interested in is whether the proposed book is a viable commercial project.

For this reason your proposal has to be more than a description of what the book will cover. It has to demonstrate that there is a market for the book by saying what sort of people will buy it and how many of those people there are (xxx thousand people bought badminton racquets last year; xxx thousand people joined badminton clubs, etc.) and to back up these statements with details of the source.

It has to state why people will want to buy your book rather than any other book on the subject. In marketing terms, this is known as USP – unique selling point. If you've managed to hit on a topic that hasn't been covered before, your proposed book will be the only one available, but in general it's a case of 'my book will cover the topic in a way that none of the others does', which means, of course, that you have to carry out the task of checking on all the competition and putting your findings on paper, including the number of pages and the price of these competing books.

If what you are proposing is a book to fill a gap in a particular series, this USP is less important, but in all other situations you need to show that your book has the virtue of originality. It may be a new 'power grip' that you've devised, or a series of mnemonic mantras for each stage of the game, or it may be that you're offering a complete run-down of the game from absolute novice to Olympic standard, when all the other books cover only one level. If your book doesn't have originality, it's just a 'me-too' and unlikely to sell enough copies to justify its publication.

Some writers include a sheet of reader benefits in their proposal. Headed 'After reading this book, readers will be able to...' it lists the major things they will have learned. Some brasher publishers will actually list these benefits on the back cover of the book, or use the most impressive as a sort of list sub-title. It's quite common in America but less so in the UK. Obviously this only applies to certain types of how-to books – you wouldn't want to do it for a book on music appreciation or comparative religions.

Although you don't want to alienate the marketing people by telling them how to do their job, it does no harm to mention any special sales outlets which might be stocking the book. You might know of a franchised sports equipment business which sells out of sports clubs, or a mail-order supplier who is interested in books. Or you might spend much of your own time lecturing to audiences who would buy the book if you had some available. There's nothing like the thought of a captive audience to brighten a publisher's day!

Three final things which actually need to go at the beginning – a title, the genre, and the length of the book.

The title, like the content of the book, needs to be original (unless it is for a series) but also needs to indicate the content. 'Badminton – the whole game' does, as does 'Grip Tight! – a winning approach to badminton using the Power Grip'. You don't need to agonise too much over the title at this stage. All titles are considered to be working titles until quite late in the publishing process, and some writers actually put 'working title' in brackets after the title on their proposals.

You may not need to state the genre if your title makes it clear, such as 'Badminton – the whole game'. Otherwise you need to say something like, 'A popular guide to Beethoven's early symphonies'. 'Popular', incidentally, is publisher-speak for 'beginners', used because the buying public doesn't like to admit it is in that category and won't buy books which use that word on the cover.

How long will it be? Easy: the same length as all the other similar books in that publisher's list, and about the same length as the competing titles. This might strike you as an odd way to decide a book's length, but there is a practical reason for it. The number of words in a book, together with the number of illustrations and such back matters as appendices and indices, dictates the number of pages, and that dictates the cost of production, which in turn dictates the recommended selling price.

Publishers know from experience that there is an optimum price the public will pay for books on various topics. If the norm for a book of the type you are proposing is, let's say, £20, readers will not be prepared to pay £25 for your book even though it contains 200 pages instead of the usual 160.

Your proposal should also indicate how many illustrations will be needed, so you can either quote the length as so many thousand words (usually to within 5,000, i.e. 45,000 or 50,000 rather than 42,000 or 48,000) plus xx pages of illustrations; or you can say 'approximately 130 pages of text plus 12 of illustrations and 12 of back matter'.

Outlines

Having seen from the proposal that your idea for a book is worthwhile, the sponsoring editor will finally look at the outline to see whether the content you propose is in line with the firm's norm, as well as being logical and complete.

The outline should be written to show, chapter by chapter, what you intend to cover. The chapters should all be roughly the same size, so each chapter entry in the synopsis should occupy the same number of lines. You may have to break some of your topics down into smaller segments to avoid giving the impression that some are short and others long.

It should end with a brief list of the back matter: appendices, bibliography, index and so on.

Producing an outline at this stage does not always commit you to producing the book in exactly that form. However, some American publishers may want to enshrine the outline as part of the contract, but most publishers understand that what you think you want to say before you start writing may not be the same thing as what you find you have to cover when you are writing. As long as the finished version of the book isn't totally different from what you proposed, nobody is going to mind too much.

Appendix A contains the outlines for this book. As you will see, the second version is greatly expanded from the first, because the first outside reader felt more detail would be appropriate, and mentioned some items which weren't mentioned in the first version (although I had intended to cover them). Compare the two outlines against each other, and then compare the second one with the main body of the book itself. You will see that a lot of topics have moved from the chapters where I originally thought they should be, mainly because the flow of what I was writing suggested a better place for them. You will also notice that all examples given in the synopsis are of UK publishers and magazines as I wasn't aware at the time that this book would be published internationally.

Putting it all together

All of this is going to add up to a fair amount of paper. It is a fact of life that even the most careful person can drop a batch of paper, and that loose sheets will work their way under the furniture. So common sense requires that you number all the pages, as well as put the title and your name, and the fact that it is a proposal, on each sheet.

Don't bind them or staple them together. The sponsoring editor isn't going to put all of it in front of the acquisitions committee, most of whom have neither time to read through a big wodge of paper, nor interest in the bits which don't concern them.

You can make their job easier by providing a page listing the contents of the outline and proposal, and also a single sheet summary of each. Then they need do no more than circulate the summaries with a brief memo stating that the readers agree with the opinion that the book is viable and that you should be commissioned to write it.

By now you may be asking, 'What has all this got to do with writing a book? I want to write, not do all this.' But you have to plan your book at some stage, and you also need to know yourself if there really is a market for it. All you are doing by writing a proposal is setting this information out in a form that will convince a publisher, instead of keeping it in your head. If you can't convince a publisher that it is viable, you don't have a book to write, so make up your mind that you've got to do a good selling job on it.

Return postage

Most books on writing tell you to send return postage. As I've already mentioned, I don't. I can see the point if you're sending in a full typescript on spec, but as I've already explained, there is no reason to do that and many reasons not to.

So you have to ask yourself what it is that you want returned? It could only be items which you might want to re-use by sending them on to another publisher, and so little of a proposal can be re-used without rewriting it that you might just as well spend the postage money on new copies. If the publisher isn't interested, they'll write and say so whether you send postage or not.

Sample chapters

Some writers include a sample chapter with proposals. I don't, waiting instead until I'm asked for one.

Many publishers don't ask. I always offer to send examples of my published books as proof that I can write decent prose. Some publishers like to see this, others just accept that my list of published books is proof enough.

The main reason I don't write a sample chapter to go with the proposal is that it has to be angled to meet the style and other requirements of that publisher. It is not unusual, even for an experienced writer like me, to have proposals turned down, and I do not want to waste my time rewriting a sample chapter as well as other parts of the proposal.

Rewriting it? Yes, of course you have to rewrite your proposal for each publisher. Just as you have to reorder your CV to bring the relevant work into prominence, so you have to reorganise your proposals to bring them into line with the individual publisher's list. The changes may be as minor as reordering the chapters or you may need to change the emphasis of some aspects of the subject or even drop some altogether. Whichever it is, if you do the book equivalent of sending bacon sandwich recipes to *The Jewish Chronicle* you shouldn't be surprised when they say no.

Incidentally, don't assume that a sample chapter written to persuade a publisher to buy will slot into the book unchanged. What you are writing is a selling document which has to stand on its own, which means you have to say things in it for clarity which will be out of place in the book itself, or which have to go somewhere else. My experience is that it is such a pain to mess about with a sample chapter, cutting and pasting to slot the relevant bits in where they should be, that in the long run it is easier to scrap it and just write the book from scratch.

Multiple submissions

Most books on writing tell you not to make multiple submissions. Publishers don't like it, they say. My view, and that of most other professional writers, is that publishers aren't going to know unless you tell them or do something like photocopying what you send instead of reprinting the whole thing. Anyway, since each version should be properly targeted, they have to be individually printed.

The reason for these two views is that publishers would prefer you to be in a position where you can't compare two or more rival offers, and most professional writers like to be able to do just that. If you have an agent, they will offer your books to several publishers at once, so there is no reason why you shouldn't do it yourself.

Things to do

■ Create a writer's CV for yourself. Where possible, use phrases like 'a regular contributor to *Suchandsuch Magazine*'. If you can't list actual writer's credits, list relevant qualifications in your subject.

■ Get hold of a sample of half a dozen books from each possible publisher and analyse them for length, illustration content and general structure.

■ Take your favourite non-fiction book and write an outline of it. Now do a preliminary outline of a book you feel you could write.

■ Prepare a proposal, including information on the size of the potential market and details of the competition.

■ Using publishing trade magazines and publishers' catalogues, compile two lists of all the companies who publish books on your subject. One list should be all the series titles, the other the non-series titles. Now ask yourself what's missing, in three categories: missing from all the lists, missing from any given publisher's list, missing in a form in which you'd like to see it.

7 | PUTTING IT TOGETHER

Getting and developing ideas

Another of the odd questions which people ask writers is, 'Where do you get your ideas?' The reply is usually on the lines of, 'The world is full of ideas – far more than I could ever write about'. This doesn't help if you really want to know, so I'll get straight to the point and tell you how to develop your own idea-spotting ability.

Finding ideas

The whole thing about looking for ideas is that you have to train yourself to be aware of them when you do come across them. Just as a cartoonist looks at the world through eyes that have been tuned to see ridiculous situations, so writers have to tune their senses to accept input that, with just a little work, can be turned into money-making text.

I've already mentioned that one of the best ways to find saleable ideas is to look for gaps in the coverage of your specialist subject. An expert or an enthusiastic beginner finds this easy and it's actually easier for the newcomer to find these gaps. I've done it myself many times, when I've been trying to find information for personal reasons and discovered that it wasn't readily available.

It was when I was clawing my way up the promotion ladder at work in the early 1980s that I discovered that although there were many books for would-be managers, much of what they covered didn't apply to women and none of them covered the uniquely female problems. There were a few academic studies of women in management, but nothing that actually said, 'This is how you do it if you are female'. By the time I'd found out all I wanted to know myself, I had enough material to persuade a publisher to publish the book, and the result was my first non-horsy book *Climbing the Ladder - how to be a woman manager*.

While I was doing some additional research for that book, I became aware that there were no books written for women on running a business. It wasn't long before I persuaded the same publisher that I should write *How to be a Successful Businesswomen – working for yourself*. And while I was researching that one, and in particular the bits on the art of salesmanship, I found, surprise surprise, that all those books assumed that the reader was male. The result was the third book in the series; *The Super Saleswoman*.

It's not just gaps in the coverage that show up during research. If you are alert to possibilities, you come across them all the time. I went to interview apricot farmers in southern France and found that they also grew artichokes; went to check out a particular hotel, admired the embroidery on their table linen and went on to write about the embroidery company, who mentioned that the sewing machines they use were developed to decorate eighteenth-century court dress.

It's a circular process: have an idea, research it and spot something else, research that and spot something else. All it takes is an open mind and some curiosity: What's that? Why do you do it? Who else does it, and how, and when? The more you find out about, the more you realise there is to be investigated, and that rule applies whether your interest is practical, artistic or psychological. And the more you study what publications and publishers are doing, the more these possibilities strike you, because instead of just thinking, 'Hmmm, that's interesting' you think, 'Hmmm, that's the sort of thing *Wotsit Monthly* like.'

One of the advantages of advancing years is that you have a vast store of facts and opinions and other experience stored in your head. If you are an avid reader, as all writers should be (seriously, if you don't like words enough to spend a substantial amount of time reading, why do you want to write?) you will find few situations where you don't know something that allows you to ask intelligent questions. Apply that ability to ask questions to every part of your life and you will soon find ideas coming thick and fast.

It will also help if you read at least one newspaper right through every day. At least once a week, read a paper which conflicts with your political opinion, to gain a different perspective on life. Ask yourself if any of the news stories or features left you wanting to know more, or whether any of them made you want to write a letter to the editor. Did any of the letters make you want to reply? Did any of the advertisements interest you. All of these thoughts could be topics to write about and you should cut out the relevant bits and make some notes on your reaction. Do the same with magazines.

Are there any problems in your life? Big or small, they could be material for articles or books. I have a generous bosom which made life difficult when I rode horses or jogged. My search for the right brassiere made a good article for a horse magazine. Dirty paw-marks on the kitchen floor led to a piece on doggie-doormats. A dog who used to take his hard biscuits upstairs to eat them on my bed made another piece on the joys and pains of eating in bed.

All of this is a state of mind. Once you start to recognise ideas you'll spot so many that you will have to sort out which are the really good ones.

Most writers have some method of recording ideas. I use those file cards, others use sticky notes, others carry a notebook and some carry a little pair of scissors. The results go into an 'Ideas' file for future use. Experienced writers prefer to leave ideas to mature for a while before they use them. So often what seemed like a brilliant idea when it first came to you turns out to have lost its sparkle a week later.

For this, and other reasons, it's a good idea to go through your ideas file regularly, say once a month, for a weeding and sorting session. I've heard it said that ideas have a 'half-life', losing their usefulness at a steadily declining rate. Often you will find another writer has spotted the same topic as you and beaten you to it. Equally often you will find that a sequence of varied minor ideas are coming together into something better than the sum of the parts and that's the one you should pull out and get to work on. And sometimes you will find that you have accumulated enough material on a topic to think seriously about turning it into a book.

Most articles have to be comparatively short, giving you room to develop only one idea. This doesn't mean you can't examine all the aspects of the idea, but you do need to keep a tight focus. Thinking back to that article on brassieres for large-bosomed horsewomen, I got a 1,200 word article out of it:

- ■ Two paragraphs on the actual problems of painfully lolloping breasts and bra straps that constantly slipped off my shoulders, meaning a constant need to take a hand off the reins to push them back up.

■ A paragraph on my search for a helpful corsetiere in the local lingerie shops, with some amusing asides on the naughtier items available.

■ A long paragraph on the non-effectiveness of various types of bra, including an expensive so-called 'sports bra' which was too soft to provide adequate support.

■ A triumphant paragraph on my discovery that the classic 'cross-your-heart' bra solved both problems.

■ A final paragraph telling of the bonus discovery that a good bra had also done wonders for my balance.

In fact, while I was researching these bras I also investigated other underwear – knickers, tights, vests and so on, with a view to their insulating properties as well as comfort. There was plenty to say about all of them, but in a 1,200-word piece I could only have skated briefly over each item, ending up with a loose focus which would have been much less interesting and which certainly wouldn't have dealt fully with the original problem. In the end, I used all this information in a 5,000-word chapter in a book on the general art of riding.

I had no intention of using it like that when I first realised it was an interesting topic. It actually sat in my ideas file for over ten years before I connected it up with some other stuff on saddlery and balance and body alignment and realised that a vague idea which I'd had in the back of my mind had finally formed itself into the thesis that balance and comfort are inter-linked and essential for competence in horse-riding or any other sport. Nobody else had written in those terms, so it wasn't difficult to persuade a horsy publisher that it was a viable book: a dual example of using the ideas file and spotting a gap in the coverage, providing scope for a book.

Developing ideas

Having spotted what you think is a good idea, you need to get into the habit of asking yourself some basic questions. The first of these is whether you have seen a real idea, or just an interesting subject area. One way to test this out is to decide whether you are thinking in terms of a book, a series of articles or a single article. If it's a book, that's fine, but if you are looking for articles and you are seeing a series, you are looking at a subject, not an idea. For example, 'Crime in London' is a subject, with many ramifications, but 'London women fear to be out after dark' is a valid article idea.

Then run through this set of questions:

- Why do I find this idea interesting? Does it offer an avenue of exploration I'd like to pursue, or does it provide the answer to something that has been puzzling me?

- Would it always be interesting, or is it topical? Will it be more or less interesting in the future? Should I wait a while?

- Does it have a natural 'hook' – something that will provide an attention-grabbing opening?

- Is it seasonal? What's the likely lead-time and when should I start writing query letters? Having said what I want to say about it, is there a natural conclusion? (This doesn't have to be a moral, but you don't want to leave your readers hanging.)

With all these questions answered, you should have the basis for knocking your topic into shape. With simple topics and short wordage requirements you may feel that a little practice will allow you to run straight through from start to finish. Otherwise it's necessary to plan, listing all the aspects of what you want to say paragraph by paragraph (or chapter by chapter) before deciding whether you've got the order right.

The need for planning

I know some writers say they never plan, but just start at the beginning and go on until they reach the end. Without exception these are people who have been writing professionally for many years, and while I accept that they may believe they don't plan, I think that what actually happens is that experience has brought them to the stage where the planning is a subconscious process.

I can write a shortish piece myself without having to make preliminary notes. I still plan out anything longer than 500 words, even if it is just a few words to get the right order, but I don't have to make anything like the depth of notes I used when I started writing. Take heart – like riding a bicycle or playing an instrument, writing gets easier the more you do it.

I used to plan in a linear form, taking several bouts of juggling paragraphs before I was satisfied. Then I discovered spider diagrams, those freeform plans where you write your main topic in the centre of the paper and put all the sub-topics around it as they occur to you, connecting them to the centre and each other with lines and arrows. I've used them ever since, every time I propose a book or article, working out connections and irrelevant tangents until I can re-order the whole thing into a logical progression.

For a book I do one spider diagram to give me the chapters, then another for each chapter. For an article I usually only need one. The original spider diagram for this book is on p iv – compare it with the first outline in Appendix A to see how it worked.

Planning isn't just about deciding the order in which you tackle each aspect. It also involves rejecting anything that doesn't really belong, and deciding when an interesting side-track is turning into a false trail that will confuse the reader. And above all, it is about balance – making sure that the less important parts don't get more space or emphasis than the important bits, as well as adding the occasional mention of an opposing view, or a brief summary before you introduce another sub-topic that is part of pulling the threads together before you tie the final knot.

Writing, in non-fiction as well as fiction, is not like knitting a scarf, where you cast on and work along one row then back along the next until you have the length you want and cast off. It is more like painting a picture, where you start with a rough sketch, then block in big patches of colour with wide brushes before using smaller and smaller brushes to add the final detail.

Level and style

One of the commonest phrases seen in rejection letters is 'not quite right for us'. This means that what you have offered does not fit the publisher's concept of what will be acceptable to their target readership. The content or the language in which you have written is inappropriate to the attitudes and level of knowledge of those readers. It usually occurs because your market research wasn't deep enough; you found out who publishes the sort of material you had in mind, but you didn't pay sufficient attention to how they present that material.

Many publishers produce style sheets for guidance and some produce detailed booklets. Where these aren't available, you should get hold of several examples of recent books, magazines or newspapers from your chosen publisher and make a note of:

- the level of knowledge assumed in the readers – beginner, expert or in between
- the level of language used – simple or polysyllabic words, simple or multi-claused sentences, level of punctuation and length of paragraphs
- the formality of the language used – friendly and informal 'me to you' first person active language (e.g. 'put the drive-shaft into the sprocket, then fix it with the clamp') or formal third person passive language (e.g. 'after the drive-shaft is inserted into the sprocket it is secured by means of the clamp')
- the age of the target reader, with books for children
- political bias, if any – this doesn't necessarily mean obvious sympathy for any one political party, but should be detectable in social attitudes (e.g. is it a 'family planning centre' or an 'abortion clinic'?).

The level of assumed reader knowledge affects not only the level of language you need to use, but also the depth at which you should tackle your subject. Publishers differ on how to approach this. For instance, in the case of a book on gymnastics aimed at pre-teenage beginners you could either give a brief overview of what can be achieved in the first year, with one chapter on the basics of bar and beam work and another on ring work; or you could ignore both those aspects on the grounds that beginners won't be ready for them, concentrating instead on the basics of how to breathe and develop good balance and muscle control.

It also affects the amount of basic information you need to include. I recently picked up a book on the South Sea Bubble. Like most people I had heard about it in a general way and thought it might be interesting to know more. The jacket blurb said that it was for general readers, but when I read a couple of pages before buying it I found that it assumed that the reader had a detailed knowledge of late seventeenth-century English history, which I don't have. I read on and consulted the index before I gave up, confused over who had done what and why it mattered.

It referred several times to 'the revolution', but because that was all it said I couldn't check it or connect it with my dim memories of the period. If only the first mention had said 'the revolution of 1688' or 'the revolution which led to James II losing the throne' I'd have been happy – and bought the book. The actual standard of writing was fine, but it just didn't tell me what I needed to know to make sense of the book.

When you get to the stage of looking at books from a publisher you hope to write for, and find that what you are reading is very different from your own natural style of writing, you might be wise to look for another market for your work. It takes a very experienced writer to produce convincing work in a style that is unlike their norm. Just as it is easiest to preach to the converted, so it is easiest to speak or write to someone whose speech patterns and reading level are the same as your own.

The best writers are now considered to be those who write as they speak, and this applies to all levels. A group of university dons will discuss the life history of a prominent individual in the same sort of language you will find in a serious biography, but the average person would explain to their neighbour how to fix a broken lawn-mower in the same sort of language used in DIY magazines. Most of us are bi- or even tri-lingual in this respect; we use one set of words and speech patterns when we talk to tradespeople and a quite different set when we talk to professionals such as solicitors. You just need to choose the right tone to avoid the risk of blinding one extreme with science or convincing the other that you lack education.

It is simple enough to achieve an easy-to-read tone in short pieces. If you've only got 1,500 or 2,000 words to explain how something works, or to expound a theory and relate a history, in most cases you'll do it in fairly short active sentences. It's when you have a target of 50,000 words or more to achieve that it is easy to slip into convoluted passive sentences.

Unfortunately this can come across as pompous or patronising, as in this example: 'It remains the case that risk cannot be eliminated altogether, and, by-and-large, the higher you set your goals, the greater will be your risk of failure.' Setting aside the fact that this writer used the expression 'far-and-away' only two sentences after using 'by-and-large' which is itself a meaningless bit of padding, they took 28 words to say, 'Risk is unavoidable. The higher you aim, the bigger the risk of failure.' (13 words.)

Checking that you have got all these aspects right when you have come to the end of writing is part of the process of revision or 'self-editing', which is dealt with in Chapter 8.

Structure and coherence

The business of working on your 'picture' with a set of 'brushes' that start wide and work down to small and fine is the easiest way to develop the professional writer's skill of coherence. This means that each component part of your writing must follow the same logic.

For instance, if you are writing a biography, where the normal structure is one of chronology, starting at (or before) birth and working through the years to death, you must do the same thing for everybody involved and in every chapter. No introducing the early life of your subject's parents halfway through, no mentioning that he was a General at the end of the war then going on to say that he had met his wife when he was a Major followed by a letter to a friend in which he reminisces about his early days at officer training college, and no telling of the first meeting between him and his wife as part of the postscript covering the final days of his widow long after he'd died.

Whether it is the chronological logic of a biography, some form of spatial logic for topics such as home improvements, or the logic of causes leading to effects in science or medical writing, it must remain the same throughout, even at paragraph or sentence level.

Let's consider a book on painting. It would be divided, as such books usually are, into the different types of painting medium: oil, water-colour, acrylics and so on. Each section should have chapters which start and go on in the same order: the paint, the brushes, the canvas/paper, painting techniques, and so on. Each of these topics should be tackled in the same way, starting with a discussion of the types available – which is most suitable for beginners and which for experienced painters – the relative costs, how to store them etc.

Within each topic, each paragraph and each sentence should be structured the same way. If the first one starts, 'Oil paints made by Thingy & Watsit are the best...' then the rest must be the same: 'Water-colour brushes made of sable are the best', not 'Of the various types of hair used for brushes, camel is the cheapest and sable the most expensive.' By maintaining coherent order throughout, you are making it easier for the reader to absorb the facts.

Variations tend to creep in for the wrong reason: because you, as a writer, are getting bored with producing a series of similar sentences and feel the reader will also be getting bored. This is where you should remember that most readers use books or articles in a very superficial way, dipping into them to pick up a few facts rather than reading them right through. The less literate ones will give up because they can't find what they want without concentrating; the more literate ones will conclude that someone who can't write in a coherent way can't know much about the subject either. Although this conclusion isn't logical, it's a common line of thought: 'If this airline can't even make the seat-trays work properly, how can I trust their engines?'

There is another piece of reader illogicality which you should be aware of, which is that the value of pieces of information tend to be judged by the relative amounts of space devoted to them. If you write four long paragraphs on the importance of choosing the right sort of paper for water-colour painting, and only one on the importance of choosing the right sort of brush, readers will think that the paper is more important than the brushes, even though you have put the brush section before the paper section and opened your remarks on brushes by saying that choosing the right brush is paramount.

Structuring short pieces

Magazines all have their own preferred structure for articles, and will reject your offerings if you don't follow them. Most popular magazines like to start with 'you can do it, it's easy', rather than use this as a winding-up paragraph. They also like to break the article up with sub-heads, which means you have to tackle each section as a whole, rather than letting each bit flow on from the previous paragraph. This is partly because they like to break up the text with photographs and partly because they believe that the average reader has a short attention span. Any parts of what you have to say which are 'data-heavy' are presented in boxes or side-bars for the same reason, so you should present it like this rather than leave the job of extraction to a sub-editor. However, you still need to structure your piece in a logical order, dealing with each sub-topic from start to finish in one place.

Writing for newspapers is different. The opening paragraph tells the whole story in a few brief sentences, the middle paragraphs expand on this, and the final paragraph repeats what the opening paragraph said in an even briefer form, ending with a short wind-up sentence, such as 'The case continues.'

Again, this is partly because of the attention span of the average reader and the way people read newspapers: flipping through quickly to sample each piece, then going back for a longer look at what interests them. It is also, to a very large extent, due to the fact that the final content of a newspaper remains fluid until just before it is actually printed. If an additional advertisement is booked, or a late 'lead' news story comes in, everything else gets juggled to fit. There isn't time to edit individual stories, so they just get chopped short, making a nonsense of anything that isn't written in the 'basics first, then detail' structure.

The final points about writing for newspapers are related to their narrow column format. Long paragraphs appear as blocks of heavy black type. It needs some white space to make it look more interesting, so it is best to restrict paragraphs to three or four sentences with a total of no more than 60 words.

Long sentences are very difficult to follow when they are spread over many lines, so your sentences should be short. This means composing them carefully to avoid the choppy feel which a sequence of short sentences can give.

Narrow columns also means avoiding long words. If you can't eliminate them completely, use them at the end of paragraphs. Sod's Law says that having to hyphenate at the beginning of a paragraph means a sequence of hyphens throughout: a visual distraction that both complicates reading and irritates the editor. You may not think editors are that tidy-minded, but they do care about the way their papers look.

Datable information

With short pieces you don't have to worry whether the information you are using will date, only that it is accurate when you write it. It is when you are writing books that you have to give a lot more thought to the long-term accuracy of what you write.

It is the cost of re-setting for later editions that is the main consideration, although obviously the marketing people will be anxious that your book does not date quickly. So, as far as you are concerned, the trick is to structure your writing so that any facts which are subject to change are positioned where changing them does not mean a whole block of text will have to be reset.

For example, say you are writing about an international treacle mining safety committee. At the time of writing, there are ten members, and you want to say so. If you say, 'The committee consists of ten member countries, each of which sends representatives to the annual meetings which are held in Melbourne' and a new country joins, the whole paragraph will have to be re-set to accommodate the longer word 'eleven'. But if you change it around so that the number of members is at the end, the resetting only involves a few words: 'The member countries of the International Treacle Mine Safety Committee send representatives to the annual meetings in Melbourne. There are currently ten members.'

But you may not need to state the number of members at all. You could avoid the re-setting problem altogether by making that last sentence read, 'The number of member countries is steadily increasing as other countries join.'

If your book involves a lot of changeable facts, it is best to put these in tables or appendices which are much easier to update. You'll have noticed that whenever I've mentioned a useful organisation, the address and phone numbers are in the appendices. I could have given them in the text, but I know full well that some will change. Organisations move, change their names, or merge with others.

On a large scale, the trick is to structure the book not only so that such minutiae can go in appendices, but also so that anything else which you might want to alter in four or five years will all be in one place. For example, you are writing a book on chess for young teenagers. Your brief is to cover the rules of the game, give some sample games of increasing difficulty, and include some material on the competitive scene. The book could be written with illustrative anecdotes throughout. In the chapter on how each piece is allowed to move, you could say, 'By moving his queen in this way, Soandsoski was able to win the 1994 championships in Helsinki.'

The 1994 championship? That's a long time ago even now. By the time the book is ready to be re-printed, it will end up quoting a date that was before the readers were born. You'd need to find more recent examples for that reason alone, let alone the chance of Soandsoski revealing a set of clay feet that would render him a most unsuitable role model for young readers. So, if you want to use this sort of anecdote, you'd do better to structure the book so that the competitive scene is in a separate section at the end, and update the whole section.

If you were writing a much shorter piece on chess, say a 3,000-word chapter in a general book on board games, the problem wouldn't arise because there just wouldn't be space for such anecdotes. There would be just about enough room to tempt the readers with the thought of the glory of winning an international title, to lay out the basic moves and mention some of the classic openings and moves.

Writing for international publication

Non-fiction writing often requires examples to illustrate various points. If what you are writing is only going to be published in your own country, this is comparatively easy, although you do have to remember that populations are now well-mixed in both ethnic and religious backgrounds.

The real difficulty arises when your writing will be published abroad. Even then it is not too bad when only one country is involved, as you can choose examples from that country; but when one book or article will be read in many different English-speaking countries, you have to choose examples that will be as meaningful in other countries as they are at home. It's a fair bet that everyone in the UK has heard of Battersea Power Station, but you can't expect English-speakers in India to understand the connection between it and an escaped pig-shaped publicity balloon, or even be aware of the saying 'if pigs could fly'. On the other hand, if you do choose an internationally known example such as the Grand Canyon and need another in the same piece, you should choose Ayers Rock or the Deccan Traps rather than another American feature.

It is slightly less crucial but still important for co-edition books. These have their own English-language difficulties, such as the need to use both metric and imperial measurements, or the fact that Americans say zucchini where the British say courgette. The publishers (or packagers) will advise you on whether it should be 'courgette (zucchini)' or 'zucchini (courgette)' but they will prefer you to keep the necessity for these cumbersome brackets to a minimum.

The problem isn't so bad with foreign-language editions, oddly enough. With these, the foreign publisher pays for the translation of the text. If they want to pay the additional cost of editing the contents to localise the examples, that's up to them. The cost of this edit will be minimal compared with the cost of the translation, so is unlikely to put them off taking the book.

Things to do

■ Consult *Chambers Dictionary of Dates* (or a similar dictionary) to see what is listed for a period six months away. Do any of the items listed spark off ideas that connect with your area of expertise? Develop these ideas for specific periodicals.

■ What did you eat yesterday? Where did it come from? (supermarket, small shops, a takeaway?) Where did the ingredients come from? (which country?) How did the ingredients get to the shops? How can you be sure they are safe to eat? Would any group of people not want to eat them? Is any famous person, living or dead, known to have eaten them? Even without your having any particular interest in food or cookery, the simple question 'What did you eat?' should take you down a series of trails, each full of idea potential. List these ideas, pick two and research them.

■ Now do the same exercise with other items – clothes, furniture, cleaning equipment, and so on. Choose two of your researched ideas and outline a medium length article, say 1200 to 1500 words.

■ Write the articles, aiming for specific periodicals.

8 | REVISION

The biggest misconception held by beginner writers is that you come to the end of writing, pull the last piece of paper from the machine, parcel up your manuscript, and send it off. You can do that, of course, but it is a sure way to invite a rejection slip. More experienced writers pull out that last piece of paper and say to themselves, 'Oh well, that's the first draft finished.' Then, after a break, they start the revision process, and continue until their work is polished to the highest degree they can achieve.

You do need a break of several days to distance yourself from what you have done and allow you to apply a truly critical eye to your work. Otherwise it is difficult to change the form of words you have used – your head seems to slot into the groove it was in when you wrote the first draft, and automatically finishes the sentence as it was before.

The fact that they expect to revise actually makes the original act of creation easier for many writers. What matters is that the words should flow out of your head and onto the paper without hesitation. If you keep stopping the flow to rewrite sections and polish little bits you are inviting the whole thing to grind to a halt and lock up in the dreaded writer's block. It is far better to let it flow to the end, then go back and sort out anything that isn't perfect.

As an example, I did this with the paragraph on page 85 about writing in different styles. The original version read, 'If you find that what you are reading is very different from your own natural style of writing, you might be wise to look for a different market for your work. It takes a very experienced writer to produce convincing work in a style that is very different to what they normally write...' I was aware, as I wrote these sentences, that I had used the word 'different' three times, but did not want to lose the thread of what I had to say, so left it until I revised.

Some professional writers even make a habit of deliberately skating over certain aspects in the first draft. These include dates, locations or names. For instance, you might be writing about the development of transport and want to mention the first steam train. Everyone 'knows' that this was Stephenson's Rocket, but as you write this a nagging doubt creeps into your mind, together with the name Trevithick. Rather than stop to check, which might mean a trip to the library, you can write a couple of question marks or the word 'Check' and carry on with the point you were making. There will inevitably be other similar facts you need to double check, so you can do them all at the same time.

The best way to tackle revision is the way a good editor tackles a job. There are so many things to check that you cannot do it all in one 'pass', so you need to decide how to split up the many things you have to look for, and do each task or block of tasks on one of several reads-through. The sensible way to tackle it is to go from the general to the specific, both in checking the sense of what you have written and the elegance with which you have written it.

You will need a pencil in your hand while you read, and you should approach the task with the conviction that you are going to have to retype the manuscript. Otherwise you may be reluctant to make all the necessary alterations. Obviously this will not be a problem if you have a word processor. Do not concern yourself with spelling or typing errors in the early stages.

You'll probably want to create your own checklist for revising, particularly if you write for a specialist market such as cooks or gardeners. I have a routine for cookery books that involves going through first the typescript before I deliver it, then the proofs, several times. On each 'pass', I check a different aspect: the weight conversions, the oven settings, the order of the ingredients (should be the same as the order in which the instructions tell you to use them), whether all listed ingredients appear in the instructions and vice versa, that the proportions make sense, and that the instructions make sense, as well as the obvious things like spelling and punctuation.

What follows are some suggestions on how to tackle the job, but you may prefer to alter the order of some of the later sections to suit yourself.

Construction

I mentioned, in Chapter 7, the importance of getting the structure right in non-fiction books. You won't want to restructure the whole book at this late stage, but you may find you need to slot in another section to clarify something. As long as you don't go off at a tangent that alters the whole direction of the book there shouldn't be any objections.

Start by reading the whole book straight through. Don't do any more than make a mark in the margin if any passages strike you as jarring. In this first read through pretend that you know nothing about the subject and that you are reading it as a stranger. When you have finished, make notes on anything of a general nature that struck you.

Then start asking yourself some specific questions. Are there any bits where you've assumed some knowledge on the part of the reader and now feel you should add a little detail? If so, how can you insert the necessary information without making it intrusive?

Have you done the opposite and slotted in over-long explanations of the, 'No dear, the round peg goes in the round hole' variety?

Does your research show? Have you included all those interesting facts because you felt it was a pity to waste them? Are they all strictly relevant? Many new writers feel that to leave out any of their research is to waste those hard-won facts, but to put it all in a single piece of writing tends to make it top heavy. If you feel you should not waste any of your research, don't – just use it for something else.

On the other hand, have you checked everything, so there are no glaring errors that will show you up? Have you got the tone right? As a general principle, if what you have written is difficult to read aloud without stumbling over the combinations of words, you need to work on it some more. Non-fiction needs to be written as clearly as possible, to make its contents easily accessible even if the subject is complex or difficult. What every publisher hopes to find is a writer who can make their subject easy to understand, and at the same time convey their own enthusiasm for the subject. If the writing is dull and it appears that the writer is bored with it, the reader can't be expected to enjoy learning about it, or become enthusiastic enough to want to know more. There is no reason why you shouldn't let your own personality show in your writing, and this is most easily done in the 'me talking to you' style.

It wouldn't be fair of me to name writers whose work I find unsatisfying, but a couple whose writings are worth studying are Christopher Lloyd on gardening and Richard Fortey on fossils. The former mentions sharp stems of dead plants which lurk in the winter border to stab the unwary weeder, in a way that not only lets you know that he writes from experience but makes you wince in sympathy. The latter tells you about trilobites with such enthusiasm that you want to grab a hammer and go out to tap rocks yourself.

Have you gone off at tangents to deal with material or subsidiary topics that aren't really related to your main theme? If you're writing that book on how to play chess, it may be interesting to mention in the introduction that hand-carved chess sets have become collectors' items, but detailed descriptions of carving techniques or the materials used aren't going to help anyone play the game.

Novice writers often find at this stage that there is a lot of superfluous material which should be cut out, but are reluctant to do it because it will leave the wordage short. Banish that thought, because it is putting the cart before the horse. Follow the simple rule: if in doubt, cut it out. Professionals do not hesitate. Anyway, you will inevitably find that there are also other areas that need to be expanded or added, and the wordage will soon come back up again.

Have you said anything that will mortally offend anyone? By this I do not mean the sort of thing that could lead to a libel writ, although you have to be careful about that, too. In my early days as a writer, I did an article for a horse magazine on buying ponies, and said in it that no sensible person buys animals at local markets where they might be tempted to buy an unsuitable pony out of pity because it was being ill-treated by the seller. I made this statement because I knew of a couple of people who'd done just that, but the article drew a very sharp letter from an affronted auctioneer, saying that I had impugned his profession because no respectable auctioneer would allow vendors to ill-treat animals at markets. Fortunately the editor sided with me, but it could have been the end of my writing for that magazine.

When you have considered all these points, in as many readings as you feel necessary, you may prefer to write your second draft before you get down to the finer points of word editing.

Writing technique

Start this task by flipping though each page very quickly to look at the paragraph lengths. Are they appropriate to the target reader? Do they vary in length, or look like identical blocks of text on the page? This may not seem relevant to the quality of the content, but it can be off-putting to be presented with great chunks of solid text. Pages of text that look 'heavy' because they lack what designers call 'white space' around them often also turn out to be heavy in content and need some variation to lighten the load.

The same applies to sentences. While you insult the intelligence of educated, adult readers, as well as produce a staccato effect, by using short unpunctuated sentences all the time, even those educated readers can lose track of a succession of multi-claused, much punctuated, sentences like this one. Even more tiresome is a succession of sentences which are multi-claused because the writer has felt a need to qualify everything. It's the non-fiction equivalent of the fiction writer who uses two adjectives to qualify every verb when a better choice of verb would have needed no qualifying.

Are there any passages of which you are particularly proud, where you feel your writing was especially fine? Are you really sure they are that good or were you just showing off? If they are excellent, why do they stand out and what can you do to bring the rest of it up to the same standard?

Have you presented as fact something that is only supposition? I remember reading a biography of Mata Hari, the First World War 'spy', which included several passages telling us what she was thinking. If these had been precluded by, 'She told her friend X that she had thought...' or 'She confided to her diary that she thought...' I'd have accepted it at face value, but otherwise it could only have been the writer's invention.

Have you made any statements that imply that certain decisions have been made when this is not true? Here's an example from a magazine eulogising the beauty of wild flowers: 'What an example alpine farmers set, for each year they allow tourists to enjoy the spring and summer meadow flower displays before harvesting the hay, thus ensuring the countryside is never deprived of its rich flora.' That statement is complete codswallop. Alpine farmers are not concerned with pleasing tourists, they are concerned with getting in enough hay to feed their live-stock through the winter. If their fields weren't on slopes too steep to tow a sprayer behind a tractor, most of them would probably be perfectly happy to increase their hay yield by applying weed-killers to the wild flowers. And the flower display is a product of the fact that you don't cut hay until the grass itself has flowered, which it does at the same time as all the other plants. If the grass was ready to cut before the wild flowers were blooming, most farmers of whatever nationality would get on with making hay, and to hell with the tourists!

Have you made any other sloppy statements like this one from a gardening magazine? 'Laburnum trees are lovely but start to deteriorate relatively young.' Relative to what? Not to themselves, since they are a short-lived tree. And what does 'deteriorate' mean? Do they stop flowering, produce fewer flowers or tatty leaves, rot at the base of the trunk, or what?

Have you made any ambiguous statements? 'The thieves found the jewels where they were hidden in the warehouse.' Does this mean, 'The thieves, who were hidden in the warehouse, found the jewels' or 'The thieves found the jewels which had been hidden in the warehouse'?

Have you fallen into the trap of the 'multi-pronoun' sentence? Read this example quickly: 'One bullock broke away from the herd and headed for the woods. The rider chased it, pushing his horse to its fastest speed. He managed to block it as it reached the first trees, turning his horse on his hind legs and cracking his whip in its face until it turned.' Which 'it' is which? Which 'his' is which?

Have any superfluous words crept in? Have you mentioned that the coal was black or the grass green? Is your biography subject a tall 6′6″? Do those extra words add anything, or should you delete them?

Word choice

Have you made any Freudian slips? Here's one I had to sort out from the first draft of an article I wrote about a new French craze: 'The French have been growing more interested in growing pumpkins.' My first thought was to change the second 'growing' to 'cultivating' but then I realised it was the first 'growing' that was wrong. I tried changing it to 'getting more interested' before I realised that the whole phrase was a mess because 'growing' had arrived in my head and stuck there. The final version read 'have developed an interest in growing pumpkins.'

Have you been careful to use non-sexist language? It offends many writers that they have to use the cumbersome 'he and she' all the time, but there is no avoiding it unless you are able to say what you want to by using 'they' instead. So no 'postman', 'paper-boy', 'house-wife' or 'tea-lady'. The solution is to restructure your sentences. For example, if the sentence reads 'The postman came before 8a.m.' you can either use the cumbersome 'postperson' or say, 'The mail was delivered before 8a.m.'

Have you used the right word to convey the right shade of meaning? Sloppy word choice is another of the give-aways of the novice writer, often linked to sloppy thinking. To convey exactly what you mean to someone else, you must first work it out for yourself.

Take this simple statement: 'It was a dull day.' Without changing the structure of that sentence, or adding a lot more words, you can be a lot more precise. 'A' dull day implies that it was the first dull day, but it might have been one of a sequence of similar days, in which case use 'another', or, if it was a long sequence of similar days, 'yet another'.

Just 'dull', as in 'not bright', or seriously dark and unpleasant? How about 'hazy', 'overcast', 'cloudy', 'cheerless', 'murky', 'gloomy', 'dreary', 'leaden-skied' or 'wintry'? There is a world of difference between 'It was an overcast day' and 'It was yet another leaden-skied day.'

By using the right word, you will be able to avoid using too many, especially where adjectives and adverbs are involved. These are commonly used to qualify a badly chosen vague word, like that 'dull', or, more frequently, a verb. 'The heavy door banged shut loudly' or 'The door crashed shut.'?

Another aspect of word choice, especially those words connected with speech, is that verbs can contain a hidden comment. The problem here is the same one encountered by fiction writers dealing with a sequence of dialogue. Faced with repetitions of 'He said', 'she said', 'he said', ' she said', they use a different verb each time: 'he snarled', ' she wept', 'he shouted', 'she shrieked'. The non-fiction writer, usually when reporting an interview, tries to vary the 'said' verb and uses 'disclosed', 'announced' or 'declared'. 'Disclosed' implies that a secret is being given away (with the added implication that it relates to nefarious doings); 'announced' implies that it is the first time the topic has been aired; and 'declared' has an implied defiance. All are far more dramatic than the simple 'told me', but may give readers a completely false impression.

The moral to all this is that you should never assume that you know what a word means until you've read a dictionary definition; and that while it is all very well to use a thesaurus to enliven your writing, you should not assume that what seems to be a useful synonym has an equal meaning to the word you started with.

Have you 'cast-off' properly? This expression is used in publishing as well as knitting, and it means finishing each article or book chapter with a sentence or paragraph which winds up the whole thing. If you don't do it, your readers will be left hanging.

Word counts, spelling and typos

Having tidied up all the aspects mentioned above, it's time for a word count. The smaller the piece, the more important it is to get the wordage right. Book publishers will forgive you if you are 5,000 words short or over, but newspaper editors who have asked for 400 words mean no more than that and no less than 395. If you don't give them exactly what they need, especially if you give them too much, they will cut it for you, and they won't be too picky about how they do it. Your carefully worded piece could end up missing its crucial last sentence in the interests of squeezing it in to the allocated space.

So it's back to rewording sentences to replace chunks of words with smaller chunks. The paragraph above is 116 words as it stands. Let's see how many words we can lose without losing the sense:

'Now do a word count. The smaller the piece, the more important it is to get the wordage right. Book publishers won't fuss if you are 5,000 words short or over, but newspaper editors who have asked for 400 words mean no more than that and no less than 395. If you give them too much, they will cut it for you, and they won't be too picky about how they do it. Your carefully worded piece could end up missing its crucial last sentence.'

Now it's 86 words, says exactly the same thing and, as well as being shorter, carries more impact.

And finally, as the very last task, when you have checked and corrected everything else and are about to type the final version, are there any punctuation or spelling errors? These say two things to editors – illiterate and sloppy – labels you don't need. And don't think that you can trust your word-processing program to do it for you. Spell chequers are knot infallible. They accept any word as long as it is a real word, so not only do they let you get away with typing 'toe' when you mean 'too', they also fail to notice when a missed letter still leaves a valid word – 'to' instead of that 'too', or 'here' instead of 'there'. Spell-check by all means, but give it the eyeball test afterwards.

All of this may read like a daunting task. It may not be, and probably won't be. You will find some of the questions apply to you, but it is unlikely that all of them will. The more you write, the fewer of the beginner's traps you will fall into, and the shorter this revision process will become.

But you should never skimp it, or think it doesn't apply to you. It is this process of ruthless pruning and loving polishing that produces writing that reads smoothly. It is the one process that will do most for your chances of being published.

Things to do

- ■ Create your own checklist of things you will need to look for when revising your writing. You should know your own prose weaknesses, so include those and also other specifics relating to your subject.
- ■ Go through the last two pieces you have written and check them against this list.
- ■ Go through those pieces again and check everything that you have stated as a fact. If you find you've got anything wrong, ask yourself what assumptions you made that led you to state these mis-facts, then add fact-checking to your checklist.
- ■ Do a Fog Index test on these pieces. (This is a test of the readability of any piece of writing. See Appendix B.)
- ■ See if you can reduce the Fog Index number by changing some of the multi-syllable words. Does it make any material difference to the clarity of your writing?

9 | ILLUSTRATIONS

Many magazines and non-fiction books are heavily illustrated with photographs or line drawings. An equally high proportion of newspaper features are also illustrated with photographs. The editors have to organise these illustrations, unless you relieve them of the necessity by offering to provide them yourself.

Where magazines and newspapers are concerned, your chances of having a piece accepted are increased immeasurably by offering a complete package of words and pictures. Indeed, in some cases, unless you can provide the pics (industry-speak for photographs), your suggestions won't be considered, for instance the piece I did on the embroidery company in France. The pics I offered were of the proprietor and her family, an old painting of the company's founder, an embroideress working at the antique sewing machine and several of the finished products. There was no way a magazine would send a photographer out to Grenoble to take pics, so if I hadn't taken them, that would have been the end of the idea.

Although it doesn't apply quite so much with books, good sample pics or line drawings (if you know a tame artist) might be just the thing to convince a publisher to accept your book.

Photographs

What editors need

Editors can only use colour transparencies or black and white prints. Anything else requires such expensive work in a photographic laboratory that they won't entertain it. The only exception to this might be where you have been offered the loan of a colour negative of a subject that is essential to the story but no longer available for photographing.

Black and white prints need to be quite large, usually 20 cm by 25 cm (8″ by 10″) but 35mm colour transparencies are usually acceptable, although some magazines prefer larger format. For general guidelines on sizes, you could consult a photographer's market handbook which lists the requirements of most popular magazines.

Using photographic libraries

Obtaining pics from photo libraries isn't really your job but you may want to know what is available, especially if you intend to fill any gaps with your own pics. There are usually a number of general and specialised libraries listed in the writer's market guides. Few will be prepared to let an unknown person go and trawl through their collections, but some will send you a selection of what they have available if you give enough details. You may have to supply a letter from your publisher to back up your request. When pics are sent to you, take great care of them: you will have to pay a stiff compensation fee if they are lost or damaged. Most publishers use picture researchers to find appropriate pics from a library. You may be invited to go in and help them choose the most appropriate.

Library pics are expensive. The publisher has to pay a fee for the right to use each picture and the cost depends on the size of the reproduction and where the book or magazine will be published. World publication costs much more than for a single country.

Working with a professional photographer

In most of the situations where you work with a photographer it will be up to you to organise the 'shoot'. If you can, go to the location on your own first, so you can ask the subjects or their owners for the facts you need without the distraction of a photographer, and also work out some ideas of what pics you want. If you can't go on a previous day, do try to get there well ahead of the photographer.

Although you can aim photographers at items you feel would illustrate the points you want to make, do allow them to use their experience and artistic ability to compose the best shots. Some professional photographers don't mind telling a keen amateur what they are doing; others do and you will just have to figure it out yourself. At the very least, explain the background to your story so the photographer knows what the pics are meant to do.

I've worked with a variety of professional photographers. Most were superb and went to endless trouble to produce just what I needed. However, on one occasion I was allocated a neurotic disaster. My husband and I were subjected to several weeks of unprofessional behaviour, treated like servants, expected to fetch and carry everything, except the precious cameras which we were not allowed to touch. Every shot I suggested was declared boring, especially when there were other things around which could be used to enhance a speculative portfolio. I was discouraged from seeing the photographs and even discovered later that the publishers had been told that I wasn't to be left alone with them in their offices. At the end of it all, the pics weren't that good and never got used.

I put up with all of this because of the time constraints, but my husband and I were so fed up with the whole sorry business that we bought a camera and we have taken our own pics ever since.

Taking your own pics

With modern automatic cameras anyone can take a technically perfect photograph. It doesn't take long to learn when to change lenses and how to compose a decent picture: you can do this at evening classes. I'm not going to tell you how to take a picture, but I can tell you some of the 'tricks of the trade' I've learned over the years:

- If you have a need for both black and white and colour, don't think you need two separate cameras. You will find you rarely need both on the same day and you will soon realise that the cost of wasting half a film is minimal compared with the cost of that second camera.

- Use a tripod and eliminate the risk of camera shake which comes from hand-held shots. Sod's Law says this will happen with the one photograph you need and can't go back to take again.

- If you are taking lots of pics in different places for different jobs, such as when you are on holiday, you'll need a method of recording what each shot is. You can buy an expensive 'data back' for your camera, but it's much cheaper to use a notebook, listing the number of the film, the number of the shot and what each shot is. How do you know the number of each film when you've taken a dozen or so in for processing? Easy – the first shot you take on each film is on a page of your notebook with the number written on it.

■ Take lots and lots of shots of each subject, changing the angle, exposure and aperture (automatic cameras will do this for you with their 'bracketing' feature), even lenses. This isn't wasting film, it's increasing your chances of getting a saleable photograph, which is going to earn at least three times the cost of buying and processing a whole film.

■ Buy film with as few exposures as possible. This means less wastage if you do have to change film halfway through a roll.

■ Buy your film in bulk at a photography wholesaler. You don't want 'process paid' film, which comes back with each shot mounted, because you'll find it costs much less to mount them yourself. Ask the wholesaler where to get exposed films processed locally, and tell the processor you are going to mount them yourself.

■ Buy simple cardboard mounts for your transparencies. This is much cheaper than letting the processor do it (this doubles the cost of processing) and you are, anyway, only going to mount the pics you actually send out to editors. Cardboard mounts are the cheapest and can have captions written on them.

■ Don't ever use mounts with glass inserts, as these can break in transit and ruin the pics.

■ Buy some plastic filing 'envelopes' for your colour pics. They are easier to post than the plastic boxes, and editors can lay them on a light-box to view all the pics without having to handle them.

■ Learn to be ruthless about weeding out inadequate pics. You'll soon build up a big collection of good ones and there is absolutely no point in cluttering up your storage space with the unsaleable ones.

If you specialise in one subject you will soon acquire some more of these 'tricks' relating to that. For instance, I carry a 'beauty box' for plant photography which includes secateurs for general tidying, some fine wire for relocating flowers and leaves, a soft cloth for polishing fruit, and a spray bottle of glycerine and water to add 'dew drops'.

Each photograph you submit should have on it your name, the copyright sign, a reference number, the date and a caption. I have some small sticky labels with my name and the copyright symbol printed on them and space for a number and the date. This label serves both transparencies and black and white prints. The caption can be written on the transparency mount, but should not be written directly onto the back of prints as this can make a mark on the front of the photograph.

You will also find out that the owners of some things have a tendency to put their hand out for a fee before they will let you take photographs for publication. This isn't totally unreasonable: they've spent money building their collection of dolls' houses or creating a beautiful garden and they know you are going to get paid for the pics. And if it is an organisation which has its own photograph library, they would just as soon you used one of their pics instead.

This doesn't mean everyone you approach is going to demand a fee, just that some do. The good news is that most members of the public are only too happy to see pics of themselves, their homes, their pets, and other belongings in books, magazines and newspapers. It is polite to let them know when the pics will be published, and I usually send them a copy of the magazine as well.

When it comes to the matter of payment for your pics, you should get an amount agreed in advance if possible. For books, the number of pics to be supplied and the fee for this (plus any major expenses, like long-distance travel) should be included in the contract. For magazines, unless they have a standard fee structure, it should be confirmed in a letter. Don't forget to send an invoice.

In general, colour pics should earn double the amount for black and white, with an added 50 per cent if they are used for magazine covers or book jackets.

At the very least, you should send your pics by registered post with 'consequential loss' insurance cover. Alternatively, you can use couriers who should get a delivery note signed and return it to you. If you do this a lot, you can get pads of special delivery notes from journalists' unions or photographers' associations.

You can buy cardboard-backed envelopes with 'Photographs, please do not bend' printed on them, or you can put a piece of stiff card in an ordinary envelope and write this message on.

If all this seems rather a performance when you are only sending pics on spec, you can hang on to the originals and send photocopies. Good print shops can make prints from transparencies, or perhaps you know a computer buff with a scanner and a colour printer?

Photographs from other sources

There are two other sources of pics to accompany features and illustrate books: the subjects, and public relations (PR) agencies.

Photographs offered by their subjects are rarely suitable for publication. Unless they have been taken by a professional or a gifted amateur, they are rarely good enough technically, and even if they are, they rarely show what you want.

One of the French apricot farmers I mentioned earlier offered to lend me some truly beautiful photos of fruit ready for harvest. Alas, there weren't any of people picking them, and this was for a magazine that likes activity pictures with lots of people. I had to return the following summer at harvest time to take pics and also had to go to the end-of-harvest party to take pics of that, too. Gosh, the life of a non-fiction writer can be hard at times ...

The other source of pics is PR departments and agencies, who will usually supply them free. This sounds great, but the quid pro quo is that they want a plug in the caption. If the editor is prepared to go along with this, all will be fine, otherwise you will have to slip the plug into your text. The other snag is, of course, that you won't be paid for these pics, so you may prefer, as I do, to take your own whenever possible.

Drawings and other artwork

What editors need

Unless you are a professional illustrator yourself, don't expect your own drawings or paintings to be used for anything other than reference material for a professional illustrator appointed by the publisher. Most publishers have a house-style for illustrations, and a group of illustrators they use regularly. The techniques needed for print production mean that artwork needs to be specially prepared for printing. It's not like just producing a picture to hang on a wall.

Working with illustrators

If your topic is at all unusual, you will have to provide reference material for illustrators, or do your own rough drawings for the artist to convert into proper artwork. This doesn't mean that you have to be able to draw yourself, as you need only give an accurate indication of what's required.

For my book on report writing, I wanted an illustration to show a pictogram. I chose to use the military strength of Ruritania as my example, with a row each of knights on horseback, archers, infantry and military catapults. My artistic capabilities are strictly limited, so I did a rough drawing of stick men on stick horses, holding bows or spears, and a catapult that looked rather like a spoon on a tripod. For each row I added a note: 'Artist – These are knights on horseback', etc. The artist produced splendid silhouettes, including an accurate rendition of a trebuchet complete with a pile of rocks for ammunition. I never met the artist, just posted my rough drawings to the publisher.

On other occasions I have sent a list of the required illustrations, then discussed the detail with the artist on the phone. It is worth pressurising the publisher to pick an artist who specialises in your subject, as you can then be sure everything about the picture will be authentic. This is particularly important when your text is aimed at enthusiasts. For a general readership, any reasonable approximation of, say, a steam train, will do, but if you are writing for steam buffs about the Great Western Railway in the 1930s, then it has got to be an accurate drawing of a Castle or King class 4-6-0 locomotive.

Even specialist artists may need some help, and this is where you need to provide some reference material such as photographs or even other books. In this case you would be wise to list everything and send it via the publisher who then takes responsibility for its safe return.

If the reference material is anything other than photographs or drawings, you should insist that the artist comes to you to take any photos or rough sketches. It isn't that I don't trust them, you understand, but I have heard of embroideries coming back with ink on them and pieces of leatherwork being left in damp outhouses.

I have also spent many hilarious hours modelling for artists, especially where my horse books were involved. Standing on one foot with the other in a stirrup hoping the horse wouldn't get bored and take off, demonstrating all the worst faults of bad riders, even lying on my back with one foot up in the air to show what happens if you fall off and your foot is trapped in the stirrup; it's all part of the job.

In general I prefer to use line drawings to illustrate such things. You can spend hours and hours, and a lot of film, and still not get the shot you want. You may get the perfect golf swing with a dreadful cluttered background or an unacceptable grimace on the player's face, whereas a talented artist can show exactly what you want every time. Drawings are timeless, too, but many things about a photograph can date it, from the golfer's hat to a car in the background or even a famous building that has since been demolished.

Other illustrations: tables and charts, etc.

Some articles or books, or writing work that you do for commercial organisations, require tables or charts to illustrate them. For instance, many of my books on running small businesses have included an example of a cash flow forecast. If you write that sort of material you will know exactly what is needed and the standard formats for them. If you use a computer spreadsheet program to produce them, do check with the publisher whether they want them on a disk and if so, what sort of formatting is required.

The only other thing to be said about this sort of illustration is that if you are using a previously published example as a crib, some aspects, such as the way a table has been laid out, may be copyright.

Captions

If at all possible, you should do the captioning yourself, even when you have not provided the pics. This is the only way you can be sure the captions will be factually correct. It is perfectly understandable when someone in a publisher's art department doesn't realise that the exotic vegetable they have blithely labelled 'Okra' (a pod) is actually 'Oca' (a tuber), but it doesn't help your reputation when knowledgeable readers blame your ignorance.

Captioning isn't easy, and the longer the captions have to be, the more difficult it is. By the time you've got to the fiftieth picture of teddy bears, you tend to run out of superlatives and different ways to describe them. The trick is to use up as many words as possible in factual descriptions , for example, 'This bear was the seventh to be manufactured by the Bloggins Bearworks in Stuttgart in 1947. His body is made of pure silk moiré from the Wun Hung Lo factory in southern Shanghai province in Eastern China...'

Apart from a desire for accurate captions, writing them yourself does have the advantage of giving you an early look at what the publisher intends to use, and thus a chance to object if any of them are truly dreadful. It's you the public will blame if they are, so it behoves you to press for replacements.

Things to do

- Go through your favourite magazines and analyse the pictures. What aspects do they illustrate? Would you have chosen to show something different? Can you tell if they are library photographs?
- Do the same with some books. Are there any points which you feel should have been illustrated that aren't?
- What illustrations do you think should be in your own book? List them as though for the publisher, with notes on what you can offer in the way of reference material. Draft the captions to go with these illustrations, doing it in the same style as those in books published by the publisher most likely to take your book.

10 | THE BOOK PUBLISHING PROCESS

If you've done a good job with your proposal, as suggested in Chapter 6, you will find yourself in the happy position of being offered a contract, and in the fullness of time, working with the various departments in the publishing house. You will find it useful, when that time comes, to have some fore-knowledge of the processes involved.

Offers, negotiations and contracts

The happy day arrives, and the mail brings you a letter from a publisher which says that they would like to publish the book you have proposed. If more than three months go by and you do not receive such a letter, it is a fair assumption that they aren't interested, although you can check by sending a letter which says, 'Would you please let me know the status of the book proposal I sent to you on such-and-such a date.'

Offers and negotiations

Even if they aren't so delighted at having been made an offer that they say yes straight away, novice writers tend to assume that there isn't any room for haggling with book publishers. With very few exceptions, notably established series, you can almost always improve on the first offer, but to do so you need to understand how the publishing industry works.

Like any other type of business, publishing houses exist to make a profit. Reducing any of their costs will, obviously, increase the profit. So with the writer, as well as the printer and everyone else involved, they will try to pay the lowest possible price.

First rule: don't assume that standard printed clauses in publishers' contracts cannot be altered. They can. It's easy: they merely have to be crossed through, rewritten, and initialled by you and the publisher.

Second rule: don't assume that haggling for better terms will make the publisher withdraw the offer to publish your book. All it will do is demonstrate that you have business sense. They expect agents to haggle on behalf of their clients, which only serves to demonstrate the fluidity of those printed clauses.

If you have no taste for such negotiations, or feel that as a novice you need advice on what is possible, now is the time to find an agent to take over, or to ask the Society of Authors to vet the contract for you.

In any case, read on. Even if it won't be you doing the haggling, you should know what you are likely to find in publishers' contracts, and which aspects you can tweak to your advantage.

Contracts

You could have a perfectly valid publishing contract which said no more than, 'A will write a book and B will publish it and pay A 10 per cent of the sale receipts.' Of course, it isn't that simple, so contracts (also known as agreements) are split up into a series of clauses. What follows is a guide to some of the clauses you are most likely to encounter in your contracts, with some thoughts on areas for negotiation.

1   A description of the book. This will give the title, often defined as a working title; sometimes the genre; and the length of the book, usually stated as so many thousand words.

    If you feel strongly about the title, now is the time to make a stand, but only do so if it is absolutely crucial to the sales potential of the book. For instance *Business French for Students* might not sell as well to students if the title was changed to *Bonjour M Brun*.

2   The delivery date. You must not miss this. As a matter of professional pride I have always met my deadlines, even if it meant driving up to London in the early hours of the morning on the stated day. If something desperate, such as flu, occurs at the last minute, you would be excused being a week late as long as you warned your editor. But beware, there has been a recent case of a big publisher deciding not to publish a whole load of contracted books, many of them because they had missed their delivery date.

Some publishers are now adding a clause which says that if you deliver a typescript that needs heavy editing (by which phrase you can read 'a complete re-write'), you have to bear the cost. While anyone who's ever done any editing work can see the point of this one, it does beg the question of who it is that considers this heavy edit necessary. Like the matter of acceptability, an outside opinion should be sought and even if the verdict remains the same, you should be given the opportunity to put matters right yourself before an outsider is engaged to do it.

3   Proof corrections. This one says you have to read and correct the proofs, and also says that you have to pay if you make too many alterations. Moral – deliver an error-free typescript and this problem won't arise.

4   The advance to be paid. If you are to receive royalties, you should get an advance, although there are some types of book where they aren't available (usually high-level academic books, but there is one well-known publisher of popular how-tos which doesn't pay advances).

Sometimes the advance is split 50/50 (signature of contract and delivery of typescript, or delivery and publication); sometimes it is 33 per cent on signature, 33 per cent on delivery, and the rest on publication. My preference is for the three-way split, because that way I get two-thirds of the money before publication rather than half. The elapsed time between delivery and publication can be anything up to a year, so you can wait a long time for that last chunk, even if the publisher does not decide to delay publication.

There may be a sub-clause in this one, saying that the relevant part of the advance is payable on 'acceptance' of the delivered typescript. In this case you should insist on an outside arbitrator to rule on that acceptability; otherwise you could be at the mercy of an unscrupulous publisher with a cash-flow problem.

You should also insist on a clause that says the book will be published within a certain time from delivery, for the same reason. Anything from 12 to 18 months is reasonable, but the shorter the better from your point of view.

The advance will be calculated as a percentage of the likely royalties from the first edition (the initial print-run). They'd like to give you about 50 per cent of this; I'd like to have 75 per cent or more. I don't always get it, but I always try. I work on the premise that the more money they've paid out up front, the keener they will be to get the book out into the shops and the more effort they will make to sell it.

Advances should always be non-refundable (except in the case of your failing to deliver) and each book you write for a publisher should be treated separately – no setting the earnings on one book against the unearned advance for another.

5a Flat fee payment. Where you are getting a flat fee for writing, which is usually when you are only writing a portion of a book, or writing for a book packager, you may get an advance of some of the fee. The rest, or the full fee if no advance is forthcoming, should be on delivery, not on publication.

Where that fee is stated as being on an amount per 100 word basis, your contract should state that this means words delivered, not the number they may eventually use in the book. Otherwise you could find your contribution has been edited down so much that you receive virtually nothing for your work.

5b The royalty. This is stated as a percentage in both cases for 'home' sales. It always used to be a percentage of the retail price (10 per cent for hardbacks and 7½ per cent for paperbacks) when retail book prices were fixed by publishers, but some publishers like to make it a percentage of their net receipts on the book. Authors' organisations don't approve of this practice and suggest you should resist it. If the publisher insists, you should make sure the percentages are higher, for instance 15 per cent instead of 10 per cent.

Where paperbacks are involved, there is a trap for the unwary. You should ask for a clause which puts a good length of time (at least a year) between publication of the hardback and the paperback, because if they bring the paperback out too soon, people will stop buying the hardback and your earnings will suffer considerably. Ten per cent on hardback is, in cash terms, about three times as much as $7^1/_2$ per cent on paperback.

If you are a known personality, your royalty could be a lot higher, but as an unknown you don't have much haggling power. However, you should ask for a 'rising' royalty, which means that after a certain number of copies have been sold, your royalty increases on following sales. If you start at 10 per cent, you can expect a rise to $12^1/_2$ per cent. There is little justification for any publisher to refuse this. Much of the cost of producing a book – the design, preparation of illustrations, editing and type-setting – is a 'one-off' payment. For reprints the only costs are printing and binding, which means there is more in the pot for you.

Where heavily illustrated books are concerned, you may find you have to share the available royalty with the illustrator/photographer. This is most likely to happen when only one individual is concerned and you may also like to give some consideration to who gets named and in which order on the cover and title page. This is important for your own reputation and also because of public lending rights rules (see page 122). You can be sure that the illustrator/photographer will have a contract which includes it, especially if they are a member of one of the professional associations which offers model contracts to their members.

The other side of this is that where your own photographs are to be used, you should be paid a reasonable rate for that use. After all, if you weren't providing them, the publisher would have to pay someone else for them, so they might just as well pay you.

6 Royalty percentages will also be listed for other types of sales, known as 'rights'. These will include overseas sales, magazine excerpts or serialisation, book-clubs and so on. The publishers will prefer to deal with all these rights themselves, and they are not all as generous about your

share as they might be, for which reason most authors' agents prefer to deal with such aspects separately from the basic contract.

Whether or not you feel you should keep control of this aspect depends on the type of book involved. Rather like the business of insisting on magazines only having First Serial Rights, making a fuss about retaining such rights is only worthwhile if they are particularly valuable.

Electronic or 'mechanical' rights, which include audio and video as well as CD-ROM, are an example of this. If your book isn't likely to be used this way, there isn't much point in worrying about this, but if it is suitable, you don't want to let go of those rights without getting a decent payment for them. The sensible thing to do in this case, if it's a nebulous future event, is to cross out any stated amount and add a bit that says 'at a rate to be determined for each specific case'.

7   Accounting periods. A few small publishers pay royalties annually. Most pay them six-monthly. With computerised accounting systems, there is no real technical reason why they should not calculate royalties more frequently, but I don't hold out much hope of this happening for many years, if ever. Incidentally, although most publishers' accounting periods are January to June and July to December, don't expect to get paid until at least four months later.

8   The 'licence' to publish the book. This is the length of time you permit the publisher to publish the book. They would like it to be for the duration of the copyright. Authors' organisations think it should be for a few years only. Publishers' associations think this is iniquitous. The latest compromise seems to be 20 years.

9   Author's copies. Some publishers give you six copies, others twelve. All should give you the right to buy more at standard trade discount. Some try to restrict this to 'copies for your own use' or say 'not for resale'. This is a nonsense with a non-fiction book, especially if you lecture on your subject and have the opportunity to sell lots of copies.

10 Infringement of copyright. This clause will say that you are personally liable for any infringement of other people's copyright. It should also spell out who pays for any fees for quoting copyrighted works or using copyrighted illustrations. Some publishers take the precaution of requiring you to produce permission letters.

While it is reasonable for publishers to consider it to be your job to source and obtain permissions for textual quotations, it may not be so reasonable where illustrations are concerned. Obviously you will know source details of any copyright illustrations that you are actually writing about, but it doesn't necessarily follow that you will know as much about peripheral illustrations which the publisher's designer thinks would enhance the book. For instance, you are an expert on fourteenth-century Iberian icons and your book is on the lesser-known Moorish icon painters. You mention the artist El Casablanco, who only ever produced one icon, which is now in the Alhambra. It is reasonable for you to obtain permission to use the only existing photograph of this icon, but not to expect you to track down and obtain permissions for half-a-dozen other non-icon paintings by El Casablanco.

11 Libel clause. This one says you are responsible for any libellous statements in the book. Don't worry too much about it. Your editor will spot any dubious comments which you may make accidentally, and if really worried about them will call in a libel lawyer for advice. You wouldn't deliberately set out to defame anyone, would you?

12 An option on your next book/s. This says you must give them first refusal on your next book or books. Sometimes it even says 'on the same terms'. You should cross this one out, because it is too restrictive. If the publisher absolutely insists it stays in, change the 'on the same terms' to read 'on terms to be mutually agreed', and make it for one book only. And when the time comes, if you don't want to do another book with them, offer them something that you know very well they won't want.

13 Reversion of rights. If the publisher lets the book go out of print, and doesn't reprint within a stated period (between six and twelve months) after you have asked them to do so, all the rights revert to you. You can then sell the book to another publisher or use chunks of it in another book. It is a good idea to ask the publisher to confirm in writing that the rights have reverted, just in case of any dispute.

All the rights should automatically revert to you if the publisher should go bankrupt. Otherwise the liquidator will sell them off to the highest bidder and you won't have any say in who takes over your book.

14 Remaindering. If the publisher decides to remainder your book (sell off all remaining copies very cheaply) because it isn't selling well, they should offer you the chance to buy as many copies as you want at the remainder price.

There are many other aspects which can be covered, including the refund of your expenses for signing sessions; the size of your name on the cover, your right to approve the cover design and so on. Most authors' organisations have booklets available with advice on publishing contracts which are available to non-members.

The main thing to keep in mind when negotiating the terms of your contract is that you shouldn't just assume that the nice people you've met at the publisher's office will look after you. They will, of course (well, most of them will) but they won't be there for ever. A successful book could stay in print for decades, during which time editorial and rights staff will change. The firm itself could change hands and what was, when you first met them, a collection of charming honest people, could change into an unprincipled bunch of rapacious stinkers. Yes, of course I'm exaggerating, but if it's all down on paper you don't have to worry.

One last warning. If your editor wants you to do anything that changes what is stated in your contract, such as delay delivery, or produce fewer words, make sure you get this in writing. If you fail to do so, you could find your work rejected on the basis that you have breached the terms of the contract. I had this done to me, in my distant and innocent past, and it took a major battle through The Society of Authors to sort it out.

Working with publishers

Delivering your typescript

Everything you've read about preparing typescripts applies to non-fiction as well as fiction: two copies on only one side of decent quality white paper, readably dense print, double-spaced, wide margins, titled and numbered unbound pages, no pins or staples, and no more than two manual corrections on any given page, which doesn't mean that two on every page is acceptable.

Almost all publishers now expect you to deliver a copy of your book on disk as well as on paper. It used to be the case that you could negotiate a keying fee for this, on the basis that they would have to pay someone else to key it, but not any more. One of the things you will receive as soon as you have signed the contract is a house-style leaflet, which will include a section relating to the version on disk. This will include instructions like 'use only one space between words and after punctuation', 'show fractions by using number keys with a slash between them rather than using any fraction keys which may be on your keyboard', and 'do not underline text'.

The editing process

When you have delivered your typescript, there will be a pause while the commissioning editor reads and approves it, then passes it to a text editor who will check it for logic, continuity, and finally such things as grammar and spelling. If you are wise, you will have ensured that your contract gives you the right to approve alterations, although in civilised firms (which means most of them) they will check such things with you anyway.

Some send the marked-up typescript back to you, some send a list for you to check against your copy of the typescript. You can either respond on paper or phone the editor to talk things through. How amicable this process will be can vary. In most cases, the queries will be because the editor thinks what you've said isn't quite clear, or perhaps because they feel something would be better if it was relocated. However, sometimes a serious attack of 'blue-pencil-itis' will have occurred. I suspect this is because some editors feel they must be seen to have done the job, but you may have to be very firm about whether it stays the way they want it or the way you want it.

Before you make a major hysterical fuss, pause and reflect on whether it really matters. It is hard when someone brutalises your baby, but in most cases it won't actually make a difference. After all, the readers will never know what you intended to say and if the end product makes sense, the new wording will probably serve as well as the old.

If you really feel the alterations are wrong, make notes of your reasons, then phone the editor. I'll give you examples of a couple of times when I've dug my heels in and won. The first was my very first book – that one on side-saddle. The editor changed every reference to 'ladies' to read 'women', on the basis that 'ladies' is an old-fashioned term not suitable to modern females. I said that the whole point of riding side-saddle is that it is an elegant and feminine art and that much of the appeal is that it reminds people of by-gone times. My wording 'draw yourself up to your full height' changed to read 'sit up straight'. Try doing it yourself. You will find that my version allows you to sit erect but relaxed, while 'sit up straight' makes you hollow your back and become rigid. I pointed out that I had chosen my words after many years of teaching had shown me the results of giving the wrong instruction.

The other occasion was a gardening book. I'd written 'purple flowering pak choi' and the editor changed it to 'purple-flowering', then added a bit about 'pretty purple flowers'. Pure imagination on her part, because pak choi is a member of the cabbage family, which do not have purple flowers. The plant has purple stems and yellow flowers. I suppose I could have written 'purple, flowering' but all of my reference books and seed catalogues put it the way I did.

This editor had made so many unnecessary corrections to the typescript that my commissioning editor finally dumped her version and went through a clean copy herself. She found less than ten things she felt were worth mentioning, all very minor.

So, it is worth insisting you know best, if you really do. It isn't, if you're just being pedantic for the sake of it. That leads to a reputation as a 'difficult' author, which will work its way around the industry faster than you could think possible.

Proof-reading

In the due course of time, you'll get proofs to read and correct. This is not your opportunity to add to or alter the text; that costs money, which is the reason for those clauses in contracts which say you have to pay for excessive corrections. Some publishers still do both galley and page proofs, but most now go straight to page proofs. With colour illustrated books you may get what are known as 'blues', which include the colour pictures. This may be the point for providing captions.

There is only one way to check proofs properly: line by line, ideally with a piece of paper under the line so your eye doesn't stray. You may think that you will spot the errors if you just read it through, but you won't. Your brain tells your eyes that they are seeing what they expect to see, and you'll kick yourself when you get bound copies and see all the typos you missed. For this reason, some authors proof-read from the back to the front, comparing the proofs with the typescript.

When the book contains a lot of figures, you need to be extra careful. One useful technique is to take a calculator and just add up each batch of figures, first in the typescript and then in the proofs. It doesn't matter if they aren't meant to add up; the process of doing it gives you a figure which should be the same for both.

You shouldn't hang around when the proofs arrive, as you will only have a couple of weeks to check and return them. If you're doing the index, this is when you do it. I like to do my own indexes, because I reckon I'm the person who has the best idea of what should go in it. I prepare the list of index items before the proofs arrive, so all that is left to do is add the page numbers. Some word processor programs have an indexing feature, but I find these more cumbersome than doing it manually. It's a bit of a pain, but I consider it part of the job.

When reading the proofs, don't omit any part of them. I can guarantee that not only will there be a bad typo in the copyright or expert assistance acknowledgements section, it will be the name or qualifications of the most difficult individual. Nor is it unknown for typos to creep into the library cataloguing information at the very beginning, or for your moral rights assertion to have been forgotten.

Watch out also for unexpected names to creep onto this page. With illustrated books, it is not unusual for there to be a list of such people as the designer, series editor and so on, but I was surprised when the name of the freelance text editor appeared on one of my horse books. I insisted that it be removed, as not only did I see no justification for it, I didn't like the fact that it implied that I need heavy editing.

On to publication day

Meanwhile, various other things are going on at the publishers. The art department will be organising a cover, which they may offer for your approval. They and the designers will be working on the illustrations. The more illustrations, the more likely you are to be involved, and the earlier that involvement may be. You may even be shown page layouts and given precise wordage allowances for each topic, so that text and relevant pictures stay together.

You will have been sent an author questionnaire to fill in, with spaces for a brief biography and possibly for a cover blurb. There's a particular delight for me in writing this blurb. Not that I think I am particularly gifted at it, but I am aware that many book reviewers do not have time to read all the books they review, and just use chunks of the blurb instead. This means that I am writing my own reviews, so naturally I use this opportunity to say how brilliant the book is!

This questionnaire will also ask for details of bookshops in your area so the marketing people can try for a 'local author' promotion; and also for a list of local papers and specialist magazines that should be sent review copies.

As publication day approaches, you may be invited to talk on radio, possibly even appear on television, and be interviewed by journalists. The best advice I can offer you in any of those situations is to enthuse about your subject as well as about the book itself.

Public Lending Right (PLR)

Some countries have PLR schemes, consisting of a payment which you receive from the government to recompense you for people borrowing your book from libraries instead of buying it. It won't be a vast amount of money, but to we starving authors, every little helps, and apart from sending in another form every time you have a new book published, you don't have to do anything. You get paid once a year for all books published and registered up to the end of the previous year.

For full details and the relevant forms, apply to the PLR office at the address in Appendix C.

11 | SELF-PUBLISHING

It may seem odd, in a book with a sub-title of 'and getting published', to suggest that you publish yourself. However, there are some situations in which doing this is advantageous. But before I tell you about those, I should first give you a definition of self-publishing and a warning about vanity publishing.

Self-publishing is when, as well as writing the book, you also do all the things a publisher would do – the design, illustrations, typesetting, printing, binding and selling.

Vanity publishing

Many novice writers fall victim to 'vanity' publishers. You may have seen the advertisements saying 'Manuscripts wanted' or 'Publisher seeks authors' which these firms place in the book sections of national newspapers. But they are not publishers at all, merely printers, and expensive printers at that.

Their routine is usually to print a couple of thousand copies, but only bind a hundred. They don't market them, or advertise them, or send out review copies. You will have to do all of that, and when you have sold all the copies you have, and ask for more, you will find they want you to pay another fee to have the next batch bound. Some even ask for a warehouse fee, and threaten to dispose of the stock if you don't pay. But if you care to pay for delivery, they will send you the un-cut, un-collated and unbound sheets.

And there is nothing you can do about it, because it's all in the small print in the contract.

Self-publishing

When to self-publish

Most of the situations when you might think of publishing yourself are those where your book won't sell enough copies, or won't sell them quickly enough, to be attractive to a trade publisher:

■ Subjects which are extremely localised, such as town history or tourist and leisure guides.

■ Subjects which have a widely spread audience but are extremely specialised, such as minority sports or obscure collectibles.

However, there are some other situations which do not require a lot of design input and which sell so easily that you might just as well keep the publisher's share of the profit for yourself:

■ Mass market subjects which will appeal to people who don't normally frequent bookshops but who will buy books through the mail. Self-help guides to better health or money saving/making are top of the sales lists here.

■ Subjects where you have a personal captive audience through your activities as a teacher, public speaker or business consultant.

■ Other topics which fall between the ultra-specialised and mass market audiences, but which can be sold by mail order. Typical examples include arcane financial subjects like trading on the futures and options markets, or small business opportunities like importing and selling oil paintings.

The self-publishing process

First you need to write the book. Whether you have published previously or are a beginner, it is often advisable to let an experienced editor cast an eye over it. Look for their adverts in publishing trade magazines or any of the writer's magazines.

Then you need to think about illustrations. Colour is expensive to print, black and white photographs or line drawings less so. Which, if any, you need depends on your subject. For instance, local history usually needs photographs, but you may be able to make do with good drawings. Sports topics are often better dealt with in drawings. Some business books need charts and diagrams, others don't need any at all. Decide which illustrations are essential and which are merely decorative, then take samples to your friendly neighbourhood computer typesetters and printers for some estimates.

You'll get two figures. The first is the cost of producing the film, which is a one-off cost. The second is the cost of printing and binding. The more copies you have printed and bound in any run, the less each copy will cost.

The cheapest way to do it is to choose a paperback with a plain white or single colour cover, with the title and your name in one colour of ink. If you've ever bought any of those mail order books which are advertised in the Sunday papers, you'll know that this is the norm. For anything else you would be wise to consult a book designer, who will know comparative costs as well as how to make your book look attractive. In all cases, get several estimates for comparison before making a decision.

Your typesetting costs will be cheapest if you can produce a disk. If you are computer literate, you might think of investing in some Desk Top Publishing software and doing the layout and pictures yourself. You should be able to buy this software and get some training on how to use it for about the same cost as getting your first book typeset.

When it comes to decision time, prudence suggests a small print run, maybe as little as 100 copies. You should be able to get the first 100 copies of a simple 120 page, text-only, paperback for an all-in sum (including typesetting) which will allow you to sell them for the same price asked in the mail order adverts and just about break even if they all sell. How well they sell will tell you whether it's worth having more printed and how many. The cost of the second and subsequent print runs will give a smaller unit cost because you won't have the typesetting cost.

It is a good idea to keep the film yourself. The printer may offer to keep it for you, but that prevents you shopping around for a better price, and it is, anyway, best to keep such things in your own hands. Small printers sometimes go out of business in which case you may have problems in recovering your film.

There are a couple of 'official' things you have to do when you publish a book. The first is to obtain an International Standard Book Number

(ISBN) and the second is to send free copies of your book to the national library and some other libraries. Check with your local writers' organisation on how to do this.

Pricing and selling your book

Most publishers price their books at five or six times the production cost, which is why standard-sized books all tend to cost the same price. If you intend to sell your book through bookshops, you will have to set the price at the same level as similar books. As far as selling through bookshops is concerned, the logistics of packing and delivery, as well as the sales potential for your books, means the only ones worth approaching are either those which are local (for books which will sell only to a local audience) or those which specialise in the subject matter of your book.

For other selling methods, you should consider the rarity value of the information you are offering. Many mail-order sellers of business books charge – and get – three or four times what the equivalent-sized book would cost from a bookshop.

Branches of big bookshop chains will expect you to give them the same large discounts that they get from other publishers. They, and specialist shops, may want to stock your books on a sale-or-return basis. You'll have to spend time on monitoring this situation, and you may find that the copies they do return are not in good enough condition to sell elsewhere.

All in all, not a very satisfactory situation. It's far better to keep control and sell your book by other methods.

The lady who writes and publishes history books about the town I live in tells me that when she brings out a new book, she pays for a 'flyer' leaflet, complete with an order form, to be delivered with the local free newspaper, and finds this an effective selling method.

If you already lecture on your subject, you will be aware that your audiences would buy a book that expanded on what they've heard. If you are an expert, and you haven't thought about speaking to audiences, think about it now. The fact that you've written a book gives you all the credibility that you need.

There are many organisations, such as ladies' lunch clubs, which are constantly looking for speakers. They pay a respectable fee, and don't mind you selling your book after you've spoken.

Other self-publishers opt for mail-order selling. There are various ways to do this:

- Direct mail-shots, where you send a letter and order form to a list of potential buyers. You buy this list from a list broker, specifying that you want names of people who are either known to be interested in your subject or who are known to have bought books by post.

- Placing display advertisements in appropriate magazines. When people enquire, you send them more or less the same letter and order form as you would use for the mail-shot.

- Display advertisements which contain enough information about the book to make people send for it straight away. This is known as 'off the page' selling, and it can be very effective. You will have to join your country's mail order protection scheme as your advertisements will not be accepted by periodicals unless you are a member.

For more information on mail-order publishing, I suggest you read Alison Cork's book *Selling Through The Post* (Piatkus).

* * *

Postscript

Throughout this book I have listed my successes as a writer, not to boast of how clever I am, but to show you what is possible. Of course I've had my failures, and of course I look back on some of the things I've done in the past and cringe at my naivity. I don't get a commission from every magazine editor I query, and I don't get a book contract from every proposal, but I am earning a decent living from my writing, and I'm much happier doing it than I ever was when I worked for someone else.

It can be done, and I hope that my experiences and advice will help you to do it too. What else can I tell you? Only what I've heard referred to as 'The six golden rules of writing' – Read, read, read, and write, write, write.'

APPENDIX A – MY PROPOSAL

PROPOSAL

by Janet Macdonald

Writing Non-Fiction – Approx 50,000 words

Non-fiction is an area of writing which is much easier to enter than fiction and one where publishers and editors are happy to encourage new writers.

For short pieces there are thousands of newspapers, magazines and newsletters, all constantly seeking material. For longer work, there are hundreds of book publishers also constantly seeking material. For writers with an interest in business or education there is work to be done on publicity, technical or training material.

Not only is all this work available to experienced or novice writers alike, it is generally more lucrative than fiction. Better still, where books are concerned, up-front payments for as-yet unwritten books is the norm.

Finally, for those writers who do want to write fiction, it is possible to turn research findings into articles or non-fiction books, thus earning some money while polishing the more creative work. Many fiction editors will give precedence to writers who already have a track record of publication.

This guide will help both beginner writers and experienced writers from the first steps of entering this rewarding market all the way to developing a reputation as a professional writer. Written in a friendly 'me to you' style, it will include examples from personal experience, with tips on beating the specialist writers' 'Mafias' which exist in every field; producing proposals which will bring advance payments; choosing the right outlet for any given piece of work; and the art of rewriting material for additional outlets.

Writing Non-Fiction
Synopsis for a book in the **Teach Yourself** series
by Janet Macdonald

Introduction
Why write non-fiction? Size of available market, articles and books needed at all levels.

1 Markets and what qualifications are needed
Specific markets - a brief look at some of the possible topics, including 'How Tos', education, sports, health, recreation, business, and many more. Importance of market research and a professional approach. Writing ability more important than formal qualifications in the field, levels of expertise, the 'Zulu' principle.

2 Getting organised
Subject research. Filing systems and databases, using the Internet, essential reference books, society memberships, notebooks. Essential equipment – typewriter or computer, printers, faxes, etc. Business records – accounts, tax expenses, submissions book. Letterheads, business cards, CVs, brochures for business clients.

3 Articles and other short pieces
Market research. Magazines, part-works, newspapers. Syndication. Regular columns. Approaching editors, enquiry letters, cuttings. Importance of lead times. Writing for businesses. Rights, fees, invoices.

4 Books
Market research. Originality and USP. Overseas editions and associated writing constraints. Proposals for non-fiction books. Original concepts, series. Agents, packagers, multimedia.

5 Level and style
Target reader – beginner or expert. Choosing the right style. Revision, getting the words right, misleading statements, clichés, 'active' voice.

6 Illustrations
Photographs, drawings, charts, etc. Captions.

7 The publishing process
Contracts.Working with editors and designers, covers, proofs, publicity, PLR.

8 Self-publishing
Avoiding vanity publishers. Good opportunities for specialised subjects. Quotations, choosing printer, production, ISBN. Marketing your own book, selling by mail order, MOPS.

"**Writing Non-Fiction**"
Synopsis for a book in the **Teach yourself** series
by Janet Macdonald
(2nd version)

1 Introduction

Why write non-fiction? Percentage figures for non-fiction/fiction books and magazines. Fiction market is highly subject to fashion, but there is always a need for information at all levels, from simple educational information for children to erudite information for scholars.

Many editors are prepared to take a chance on writing ability if your expertise fits their needs. Fiction editors are not – you have to prove you can write.

Non-fiction books are usually commissioned from no more than a proposal and sample chapter – this means a contract and immediate money. Your first fiction book has to be complete before anyone will consider it.

With shorter pieces, there is an inexhaustible market for articles, but the market for short fiction is almost non-existent (except women's magazines).

Why waste your research for a fiction project when you can also use it to write articles or non-fiction books?

What to write about – how to spot gaps and develop saleable ideas. Topics to avoid.

2 Markets and what qualifications are needed

Specific markets – a brief look at some of the possible genres, including 'How Tos', textbooks, sports, health, recreation, business, travel and food, art and music appreciation, history in all its forms, religion, psychology, health, biography or ghost writing – and many more.

Markets are there – editors need 'product', especially when they are in a new job. Look for these situations – *Bookseller, UK Press Gazette, Media Guardian*, etc.

Importance of market research and a professional approach – anything else is a waste of time. Publishing world is full of naive wannabees and all editors have a deep scorn for them, so tips on avoiding this label. Your aim, whether writing short or long pieces, is a long-term relationship with an editor– repeat business is easier to get than new.

Writing ability more important than formal qualifications in the field, what counts is level of expertise. How would you describe yourself in the blurb? The 'Zulu' principle – general interest books on popular topics now sell best if written by TV personalities, so forget them and concentrate on getting a foot in the door by being an expert on something obscure (author's own experience – side-saddle).

Do you need an agent? Pros, cons, finding the right one.

Non-publishing markets – small and large business, colleges and other training organisations.

3 Getting organised

Subject research. First step is to establish a filing system or database. Your system must include sources of all information and a method of showing what is direct quotes or your own précis and comments. From simple systems using old envelopes to complex computerised databases.

Using your local libraries – reservation systems, inter-library speciality system. Other libraries – colleges and universities, professional bodies, museums, etc. Other sources of information – Internet, commercial organisations, private collections (and letters), closed interest groups and societies, public records, newspaper libraries. Using professional researchers, students. Other (non-professional) sources of information. Interviewing techniques.

Importance of going back to the primary source. Dangers of making assumptions – need to check and double check. Difference between research and plagiarism. When you need permissions for quotations.

Building your own reference library – standard writer's reference books, your own speciality. Building a chain of contacts, society memberships.

Other elements of creating your own office and the business of writing – essential equipment – typewriter or computer, printers, faxes, etc. Importance of presenting a professional image. Business records – accounts, tax expenses, submissions book. Letterheads, business cards, CVs, brochures for publishers and business clients. Sending an annual reminder that you exist – editors change.

4 Articles and other short pieces

Market research. Magazines, part-works, newspapers, Web pages. BRAD, *Writer's and Artist's Yearbook*, others, big branches of W H Smith, etc.

First check if they use freelances, then ask for editorial guidelines and style sheet, plus index of recent topics. Advertising department will send sample copy. Choose magazines carefully, many start up and close down quickly. Advantages of working for group magazines (e.g. EMAP).

Newspapers – locals sometimes want specialist columns, but pay badly. Dailies occasionally take pieces from freelances (e.g. *The Times*) but colour supplements rarely do unless you are in the right social circle.

Part-works – craft and other special interest topics (e.g. steam trains) always want material.

Contributions to book projects (e.g. *Country Life Book of Saddlery*).

Approaching editors (finding out who to approach), enquiry letters (don't phone, do fax), cuttings. Importance of lead times. Structure your suggestion for the publication. Regular columns. Fillers. Delivering the MS and disk. Meeting deadlines, reporting problems in plenty of time.

Writing for businesses – their brochures, handbooks, training manuals, reports, in-house magazines and newsletters.

Rights, FBSR, all rights. Syndication. Selling abroad. Converting series of articles to a book.

Fees, NUJ and other rates. The 'good, fast, cheap' triangle ('you can have any two...') Hourly rates for business writing. Asking for a rise and other negotiations. Getting paid – invoices, reminders, talking to the accounts department.

5 Books

Market research. *Bookseller*, *Publishing News*, London Book Fair. Big bookshop for overview, then publishers' catalogues. Specialist bookshops (e.g. Books for Cooks).

Choosing the right level of publisher. Original concepts, series. Small publishers better for beginner writers. Packagers.

Proposals for non-fiction books (sending them to the right person) – the proposal, the synopsis (or outline), the covering letter and your CV. Structuring the synopsis – a mixture of your own logic and whatever standard approaches seem to apply to your chosen publisher. (Yes, this means rewriting it for Publisher B if Publisher A turns it down.) Numbering and dating later versions of proposals.

Originality and USP.

6 Putting it together

Getting and developing ideas. 'Hooks' for short pieces, unique angle or series approach for longer pieces or books. How ideas grow out of other ideas (author's own experience).

Structure and coherence, need to take reader from beginning to logical end, regardless of length and genre. Structure applies at all levels – whole book, each chapter, paragraphs. Ditto coherence – all the way down to sentences.

Ways to present information and organise material, use of spider diagrams as structuring tool. Need to structure books with reprints and updates in mind. Overseas editions and associated writing constraints.

Examples:
- 'Playing Chess' – as a 3,000-word chapter in 'Board Games' book and as a 50,000-word book for children.
- 'Henry Bloggs – 19th-century novelist' as a 1,000-word article for a county magazine, as a 5,000-word article for a history magazine, as a 100,000-word biography.

Other matter – bibliographies and acknowledgements.

7 Level and style

Choosing the right style – why it's important. Ask for style sheet, checking published examples from chosen publisher.

What is style? – letting your own voice come through. Avoiding patronising the reader, or being over formal – formality leads to pomposity. Style should be appropriate to genre.

Level – is target reader a beginner or an expert? Depth of coverage - what to include and what to leave out. Language, voice and tone. Dangers of false assumptions. Emphasis and proportion.

Using the 'active' voice and other considerations of verb use.

The dreaded 'he or she' problem and other political correctness.

Examples throughout.

8 Revision

Why it's necessary, when to do it, incidental advantages, how to do it.

Stages of revision:

- major faults: construction, missing or excessive information, going off at tangents, cutting and wordage loss, offensive or libellous comments
- minor faults: paragraph and sentence lengths, variable quality of writing, misleading statements, confusing pronouns, superfluous words, repetition of individual words, clichés, 'datable' comments
- checking facts and other items: spelling of names; measurements, dates, etc.
- general spelling and punctuation. Don't trust spell chequers!
- word counts.

9 Illustrations

Photographs make magazine articles easier to sell, good sample pics may clinch a book deal.

What editors need – transparencies, prints, format. Providing your own photos, working with photographers (author's own experiences – temperament, contracts, payment), using picture libraries, using the subject's own photos. Permissions, copyright in photos.

Drawings, your own, or your need to provide reference material. Line drawings often better than photos to illustrate 'How-To'. Working with artists (author's own experiences, as above).

Charts, diagrams, etc. Choosing the right type, producing them on your computer.

Captions – who does them? Best if you do, since the readers will blame you if they are wrong.

10 The book publishing process

Offers, negotiation and contracts. Royalties and advances.

Delivering the MS – presentation same as fiction (margins, spacing etc.). Number of hard copies. Disks – when to send them, format.

Working with editors and designers. Getting changes in writing. The editing process, marked hard copy or list of queries. When to argue about changes. Proofs and indexes.

Covers, publicity.

Public Lending Right (PLR)

11 Self-publishing

Difference between self-publishing and vanity publishing. Avoiding vanity publishers.

Self-publishing – good opportunities for specialised subjects. Books, newsletters, 'special' reports.

Practicalities – quotations, choosing printer, cover design, typesetting and production. Do your own – cost of DTP courses. ISBN.

Marketing your own book, selling by mail-order (Mail Order Protection Scheme), other selling methods – lectures and other public speaking. If all else fails, give copies to libraries and collect PLR.

Appendices

1   The spider diagram and sequence of proposals for this book
2   Useful addresses
3   Bibliography

Index

NB   All chapters will be headed with appropriate quotations, and will include examples and end with exercises.

APPENDIX B – FOG INDEX TEST

This is a standard test of the readability of any piece of writing.

1 Choose several samples of 100 words and:

2 Calculate the average number of words per sentence.

3 Count the number of words with three or more syllables in each sample, ignoring words with capital letters, combination words like 'lawnmower' or 'handwritten', and words ending with '-ed' or '-es'.

4 Add together the answers to 2 and 3 and multiply by 0.4.

■ If your answer is less than 10, your writing is very easy to read.

■ 10 gives writing that can be read by the average 15-year-old.

■ 11–13 gives writing that can be read by the top 20 per cent of 16-year-olds.

■ 14–16 gives writing that can be read by first year university students.

■ 17 and over gives writing that can be read by university graduates.

Check out the Fog Index for some of the daily newspapers and your favourite magazines.

APPENDIX C –
USEFUL ADDRESSES

Writer's/Author's Organisations

Authors Guild
330 West 42nd Street, 29th Floor
New York
NY 10036-6902
USA
email: Staff@authorsguild.org
Internet: www.authorsguild.org

Australian Society of Authors
PO Box 1566
Strawberry Hills
NSW 2012
Tel: (02) 9318 0877
email: asauthors@peg.pegasus.oz.au

New Zealand Society of Authors
(PEN NZ Inc)
PO Box 67 013
Mt Eden
Auckland 3
Tel: (09) 630 8077

National Union of Journalists
London
UK
Tel: 0171 278 7916

American Society of Journalists
and Authors
1501 Broadway, Suite 302
New York
NY 10036
USA
Tel: (212) 997 0947

Society of Authors
84 Drayton Gardens
London
SW10 9SB
Tel: 0171 373 6642
email: authorsoc@writers.org.uk

Irish Writer's Union
19 Parnell Square
Dublin 1
Tel: 353-1-872-1302
email: iwc@iol.ie

Writer's Market Guides

These are updated regularly and can be found in booksellers or libraries:

UK, Canada, Australia, Eire and Northern Ireland, New Zealand, South Africa and USA -*The Writer's and Artist's Yearbook*, published annually by A & C Black.

USA and Canada - *Writer's Market*, published annually by F & W publications.

USA and Canada - *The Writer's Handbook*, published by The Writer Inc.

Australia - *Bookman Media Guide*

Advertiser's rate books

British Rate and Data, EMAP Business Communcations.
Tel: 0171 505 8273.

Australia Advertising Rate and Data, Thompson Publications.
Tel: 612 688 2411.

Canadian Advertising Rates and Data, Rogers Communication.
Tel: (416) 596 5860.

New Zealand Media Planner & PRRADS, Press Research Bureau Ltd.
Tel: 4385 7644.

South African Rates and Data, SARAD Publishing Co (Pty) Ltd.
Tel: 11 4785618.

USA - Standard Rate and Data Service Inc. Tel: (847) 375 5000.

Public Lending Right Office, Bayheath House, Prince Regent Street, Stockton-on-Tees, Cleveland, TS18 1DF. Tel: 01642 604699. Fax: 01642 615641.

INDEX

accounting 30
acknowledgements 36
acquisitions committee 74
advances 3, 64, 112
advertisement led magazines 54
advertising directories 50
advertorial 53
agents 20–3, 111
ambiguity 97
appendices 74, 89
articles 49–64
  payment 2, 58, 60–2
  submitting 58

back matter 74
bibliography 36, 74
blurbs 84, 121
book fairs 66
book packagers 68
brochure 24, 27
business
  cards 28
  information 44

captions 108
charts 108
children, writing for 17, 34
clichés 8
co-editions 68, 90
coherence 86
collaboration 19
columns 57
commissioning editor 66, 67
composite books 55
computers 27, 29, 30, 31, 33
construction 94
contracts 3, 110–18
copyright 37, 116
CV 13, 27, 57, 69, 71, 76

databases 33
datable information 88
delivery dates 111
delivering typescripts 118
developing ideas 81
disks 60, 118
drawings 101, 106–8

email 28
expenses 31

fax 28
fiction 1, 2, 3, 64, 83
filing systems 32
fillers 55
focus 5

gaps in coverage 65, 78, 81
genre 10, 72
ghost writing 18, 19

ideas 5, 8, 78
illustrations 69, 73, 101–9, 124
index 74
information storage 32, 35
international publication 90
Internet 24, 25, 35, 45, 46, 53, 59
interviews 35, 46
ISBN 125

kill fee 61

lead time 55, 82
length of books 73
level of writing 83
libel 17, 95, 116
libraries 42, 44

mail order
  publishers 14, 68
  publishing 126, 127

markets 4, 10–18, 23, 24, 49, 52, 60, 65
  overseas 52
moral right 38, 120
multiple submissions 76

naivity 7, 57
negotiating contracts 110

offending readers 95
office 31
on-line research 45
options 116
outlines 69, 73, 74

page numbering 59, 74
part works 54
permissions 36, 41, 116
photographic libraries 103
photographs 101–6
plagiarism 37, 39
planning 82
press
  directories 50, 54
  officers 45
printing, self-published books 124, 125
professionalism 6, 26
proof corrections 112, 120
proposals 2, 69, 71, 72
public
  archives 44
  lending right (PLR) 121
  relations officers (PRs) 45
publishers' catalogues 65

qualifications 20, 70
query letters 3, 7, 56
quotations 40

readers' letters 56
reference books 47
rejection 92
remaindering 117
research
  market 5, 6, 49, 65, 83
  topic 3, 4, 32, 33, 34–48, 79, 94
return postage 57, 75
reviews 121
revision 86, 92–100
rights 21, 59, 114, 115, 117
royalties 21, 64, 113, 114

sample chapters 2, 69, 75
sentence length 96

self-editing 86
self-publishing 123–7
series of
  articles 58, 82
  books 66
sexist language 98
short stories 1
slush pile 82, 92, 94
specialising 5, 55
spell checkers 100
spelling 30, 99
spider diagrams 83
stationery 26, 28
stolen ideas 8
structure 86, 87, 94
style sheets 84
submissions 31
superfluity 97
supposition 96
syndication 54, 59
synopsis 69, 74

tables 108
tangents 95
tax 31
telephone 28
  answering machines 28
text editing 118
titles 59, 72, 73
tone 85, 94
trade
  magazines 51, 52
  publishers 14, 67
translation 91
typewriters 29
typos 99, 120

unique selling point (USP) 72

vanity publishing 123

word
  choice 97
  editing 95
  processors 27, 29, 100
working titles 73
writers'
  block 92
  market guides 65
writing
  for businesses 62
  technique 96